GOD, I'M STRUGGLING

* Committed to the cause
not Resigned to the struggle

Let your power fall when your name is
called Prove the doubters wrong you're
still mighty and strong
So fight this battle for me and help my
unbelief So I can tell ALL of my friends

You HAVE WON AGAIN!!

GOD, I'M STRUGGLING

Lessons To Be Learned From Biblical Figures When Facing Crises.

Charles J. Pearson

Cover design: Nehmen-Kodner

Unless otherwise noted, Scripture quotations are from The Holy Bible, English Standard Version. ESV® Text Edition: 2016. Copyright © 2001 by Crossway Bibles, a publishing ministry of Good News Publishers.

ImpactfulLiving, LLC Teach. Equip. Inspire.
www.impactfulliving.net

Ordering Information:
For details, contact impactfulliving5@gmail.com.

Print ISBN: 978-1-7375171-1-5
eBook ISBN: 978-1-7375171-0-8

Printed in the United States of America on SFI Certified paper.
First Edition

Dedicated to the elders in my family who persevered through life's challenges and taught me a love of God.

Our Goal—and Its Reward

That I may know Him and the power of His resurrection,

and may share His sufferings,

becoming like Him in His death,

that by any means possible

I may attain the resurrection from the dead.

Not that I have already obtained this or am already perfect,

but I press on to make it my own,

because Christ Jesus has made me His own.

Brothers, I do not consider that I have made it my own.

But one thing I do:

forgetting what lies behind

and straining forward to what lies ahead,

I press on toward the goal

for the prize of the upward call of God

in Christ Jesus.

Philippians 3:10–14

today God is first 1/19/15

I want to know Christ and the power of His resurrection LORD, I do. I want to know you more. I want to praise you for the power of your resurrection. I want to be a living testimony of the power of your resurrection; the joy of your presence. The miracle of your work in my life. Please use me to reach the spiritually lost and needy in this world, to point them to you that they may also know the power of your resurrection and gain revelation of you and your will for all of us. Bless you, LORD; I love you. It is in your mighty matchless name I pray. Amen

Father, I thank you. I am so glad I have not followed a cunningly devised fable. I thank you for the Revelation of truth which is eternal. I pray for an expansion of vision — an expansion of revelation, a deeper willingness to go further with You than I've gone before. That I may walk circumspectly -- that if You would appear at my side, I wouldn't embarrass You, because I am walking in the place of obedience. Let Your blessing be upon me. Amen

Table of Contents

Preface

So much in life can be a challenge:

Raising your children

Choosing a mate

Breaking bad habits

Correcting a mistake that you've made

Needing to work while you go to school,

needing to repeat a class, needing to get tutoring,

staying with it and not quitting—it's all a struggle!

Starting a business

Working in a hostile environment

Life is a struggle!

This book reveals much of what I've learned from my own challenges, in addition to what I've learned from the struggles of men and women in Scripture as I've read about them and have meditated upon their lives. I've learned that God is not only present in every struggle, but also has a plan for every struggle. The book concludes with a reflection about several contemporary challenges that have had an indelible impact upon people in the United States of America as individuals, as a nation, and as a society. I believe that God's presence is clearly evident even amid those struggles, and that we will be blessed by consciously seeking to experience Him in all of our difficult times.

Introduction

"I'm Comin' Up the Rough Side of the Mountain"

The old people in Arkansas had a song they often sang on Sundays: "I'm comin' up the rough side of the mountain. I must hold to God, His powerful hand. I'm comin' up the rough side of the mountain. I'm doin' my best to make it in!" As a child, I just sang along with no real understanding of the words.

Then I heard a friend ask, "Why don't they just go to the smooth side instead of the rough side?"

An old sage replied, "There's nothin' to hold onto on the smooth side!" While the statement may seem comical, it holds a wealth of truth—the rough side of the mountain has footholds and crevices for us to hold onto as we progress.

Lifting Weights

I lift weights in order to stay fit. My goal is to be healthy. Power, strength, and overall fitness are my objectives. As I was focusing on developing muscle and strength, I soon realized that I could not become stronger by lifting lighter weights. If I did a barbell squat using sixty pounds and considered that anything more than a warm-up, then I was not going to move closer to my goal that day. In order to get stronger, I had to lift more weight; I had to do it consistently; I had to use good form; I had to add more weight in reasonable increments over a period of time.

Here's an interesting corollary: If I did the same lifts with the same amount of weight day after day in my training, I would not stay the same; I would decline in my level of fitness. We cannot maintain our current status when we cease to train, when we cease to struggle, when we cease to be challenged. If we truly want to increase our strength, we must *embrace* the struggle.

Most of us would like the road to the top to be easier. We look for the chairlift, the elevator, or the escalator so that we don't have to take the stairs. We look for the easier way.

The Power of the Struggle

By now, my premise should be obvious. My thesis is simply this: *There is power in the very act of struggle.* Growth occurs within each of us when we embrace a struggle. We benefit from the challenge mentally, physically, spiritually, emotionally, and intellectually. We grow from struggle, from the tests of life. When we have exhausted ourselves and yet push on, when we squeeze out one more rep, when we push past that fifth mile in order to finish the last two and finally feel that second wind—then we come to realize the power of Philippians 4:13—"I can do all things through Him [Christ] who strengthens me."

A Personal Struggle with Pain

Several years ago I was participating in a leadership initiative designed to bring community leaders together to tackle problems in our city, county, and region. These sessions took place one weekend a month, on a Friday and a Saturday. We covered one specific topic each weekend. One weekend we researched housing, the next weekend we studied the criminal justice system, and another weekend, science and research in the region.

On one weekend we focused on education. The entire group met in an auditorium to hear two national experts address education reform efforts. One minute I sat comfortably and listened as one presenter described processes designed to accelerate learning for all students. This would involve teachers and principals working incredibly long hours and weekends, all the while being available for students and their families seven days a week. I could feel my stress levels rising as I considered how hard this work would really be.

Then suddenly I was in pain. I stood, quickly clambered over several people, and moved to the side of the auditorium, where I could brace myself against a wall. I stood and listened to the rest of the presentation, occasionally shifting from left to right to alleviate the pain. I returned to work that Monday, but the pain continued to increase. By the end of my second day back at work, every position I took—standing or sitting—was painful.

I went to a doctor and described my symptoms. He ordered an MRI, which revealed that I had four bulging discs in my neck and upper back. The most intense pain settled in my left arm. Whenever night approached, I came to dread what I knew would occur. The pain radiated from my back to that left arm, and I couldn't sleep. I'd get momentary solace trying to sleep sitting up, partially lying back; or lying on my back with the arm hanging from the bed or draped across my chest.

No matter what I tried, I could doze for only thirty minutes; then a stabbing pain would surge through my arm and awaken me. The pain became a part of my life, of my every move. It affected how I worked, determining whether I could sit for long in a meeting or effectively lead a team. And each night I struggled to sleep. Over a three-month period, I went through physical therapy, hoping not to need surgery, a possibility my doctor had mentioned. One night I managed to sleep for an hour. Then over the next few nights, as the therapeutic sessions had their impact, I was able to sleep through the night.

I suddenly realized how precious a full night's sleep was—something I had always taken for granted. I was compelled to pray, "Thank you for that which I have taken for granted—a full night's rest." Struggle, even the everyday "garden variety" kind of struggle, can have an impact on our thinking, our outlook on life.

Ancient Struggles

Struggle existed in the universe even before the creation of man. The Bible describes the struggle that occurred in heaven when Lucifer led a rebellion against God in order to gain power. Envy was his motivation. A desire for prestige and significance was his catalyst. Ultimately, the desire for position and power led to a war that caused Lucifer to be thrown from heaven to earth—with lasting impact on the souls dwelling here.

This basic struggle was then repeated in the conflict that occurred within Cain after he presented an unacceptable offering to God. God's rejection of his offering sent Cain into an emotional spiral that eventually led him to kill his brother, Abel. The first human blood was shed as a result of this internal struggle. Rather than dealing with the consequence of his own choice to offer God less than his best, Cain made Abel the target of his anger. One brother killed the other, and senseless violence entered the world.

Why Consider This Story?

The Bible states that all Scripture is inspired by God with the purpose of equipping us to be effective believers and witnesses of its truths. If we read a story, such as the struggle between Cain and Abel, what should we glean from it other than the historical facts? Since God is always intentional, we know that the passage is included in Scripture for a purpose. We must be able to interpret what is said and then actively apply it to our lives—so that our lives, might be victorious.

I submit that if we are able to see God's hand in our struggles, to realize that His fingerprints are all over every challenge, every experience—then we can begin to learn and grow from every challenge that we face. Our awareness of purpose will allow us to become stronger during the struggle and—whether we feel that we have won or lost the struggle—to find ourselves at a higher level of development when the struggle is over.

Embracing Our Struggle

So it is with the struggles that we face in life. We must come to understand the purpose of the struggle, our role in the struggle, and how the experience of the struggle can benefit us.

Before you read each chapter in this book, I encourage you to read the passage of Scripture that is cited below the chapter's title. Then, as you read each chapter, my hope is that you'll begin to see—that you'll even begin to *look for*—the purpose of God as you face your own personal struggles.

The beauty of Scripture is its unflinching presentation of God seeking to present Himself to man, and the myriad ways that men and women have responded to Him over the centuries. We come to understand ourselves better through the Word of God. We learn that our situations are not so unique after all. Yes, our dilemmas are painful, but others have experienced those dilemmas as well. The lives of people written about in the Bible inform us, inspire us, encourage us, and ultimately teach us who we are in the sight of God.

As you read each chapter in this book, seek an answer to each of the following questions:

What was the struggle of the principal person in the story?
What did that person's struggle teach him about the nature of God?
What was the impact of that person's struggle on him?
What was the impact of that person's struggle on others?
How does that person's experience with God in this struggle relate to your life?

El-roi

Hagar: Seeing the God Who Sees Me

Genesis 16

Hagar's struggle with Sarai demonstrates that God was intimately involved in her life and had a special plan for her despite the dire nature of her situation.

Hagar's Story

God had promised Abram and Sarai that they would have a son, but years and years had passed without that promise being fulfilled. In an effort to bring that promise to fruition, Sarai—barren and now older—offered Hagar, her handmaiden, to Abram in hopes of Hagar becoming pregnant. (This was a common solution to barrenness in that time and culture.) The handmaiden would bear the child. However, the child would belong to Sarai, who would then present the child to Abram, and Sarai and Abram would raise the child as their very own.

All went as planned. Hagar became pregnant with Abram's child, but once she became pregnant, she began to flaunt her pregnancy in Sarai's face. It doesn't take much imagination to picture what this looked like or sounded like: Hagar's experiencing morning sickness, seeing her abdomen growing, calling attention to the baby's movement. As Hagar got more attention and Sarai got less, tension mounted.

Furious about the whole situation, Sarai laid the blame for this entire debacle at Abram's feet. He reminded Sarai that she had power over her servant, and could deal with Hagar in any way she chose. Sarai retaliated against Hagar so harshly that Hagar ran away.

1

This was not a shining moment for anyone involved. Bad decisions are like that. They bring out the worst in human nature, and this situation was no exception.

Reflecting on Hagar's Story

Hagar fled! When she did so, she sought to return to her old beginnings. Many of us tend to do the same thing. Turmoil often leads us to seek solace in our past, no matter how dismal that past may have been. However, in solace we often hear God's voice more clearly. Hagar's experience with this is recorded in Genesis 16:7–8.

> 7 The angel of the LORD found her [Hagar] by a spring of water in the wilderness, the spring on the way to Shur. 8 And he said, "Hagar, servant of Sarai, where have you come from and where are you going?" She said, "I am fleeing from my mistress Sarai."

Traveling back to Egypt, alone and pregnant, Hagar arrives at a spring in the middle of the desert, where she encounters God— or to put it more accurately, where God, through an angel, reveals Himself to her. During this encounter, God challenges Hagar with two existential questions: *Where are you coming from? Where are you going?*

How profound that God would open a dialogue with Hagar by questioning her. A deeper analysis of the questions helps to clarify the questions' purpose: causing Hagar to reflect upon her situation.

"Where are you coming from?" What had brought Hagar to this point in her life? What decisions had she made? What relationships had she established? What specific circumstances had driven her to this point in her life? What had been her responsibility in all that had taken place?

And then *"Where are you going?"* What decisions had Hagar made about her next steps? What had she learned from her previous experience? What baggage was she carrying into the future?

2

The two original questions reveal so much about God. God *finds Hagar* where she is—beside a pool in the wilderness. This demonstrates that God is aware of Hagar's *present*. The questions cause Hagar to reflect upon her *past* and contemplate her *future*. In one action and in two questions, God reveals His eternal knowledge of Hagar and His eternal presence with her. He does the same for us.

God reassures Hagar that He knows her intimately, calling her "Hagar, Sarai's maid." He not only knows *who* she is, but He also knows *where* she is (both physically and emotionally) and knows the state of her relationships. He knows her dilemma (alone and pregnant in the wilderness), He confirms that He knows her destiny (pregnant with a son), and then God informs her of her son's personality and of the blessings to come.

Finally, in Genesis 16: 9–13, God speaks to Hagar about what she should do next:

> [9] The angel of the Lord said to her, "Return to your mistress and submit to her." [10] The angel of the Lord also said to her, "I will surely multiply your offspring so that they cannot be numbered for multitude." [11] And the angel of the Lord said to her, "Behold, you are pregnant and shall bear a son. You shall call his name Ishmael, because the Lord has listened to your affliction. [12] He shall be a wild donkey of a man, his hand against everyone and everyone's hand against him, and he shall dwell over against all his kinsmen."
>
> [13] So she called the name of the Lord who spoke to her, "You are a God of seeing," for she said, "Truly here I have seen Him who looks after me."

Return to the situation you have fled from! There is still a future there. The relationships are not severed. Go back! Surely this would be an unnerving command—except Hagar had come to understand God, to "see"

God in a new light. Now she understood that He was a God who was personally involved in her life, a God who fully understood her, a God who cared. And in doing all of this, in enduring this period of struggle, Hagar came to *"see the God who sees her."* She came to know God more intimately as a personal protector.

I liken this awakening awareness in her to those moments in our own lives when we are faced with a dilemma, wondering what God is going to do, or how a challenge in our life will turn out. Suddenly we get clarity, and we exclaim with delight or simple awareness, "Ooh, I see! I get it now! That's what's going on! That's what this is about!" In her moment of clarity Hagar had seen God and had recognized Him as the one who sees and cares for her.

Hagar's struggle taught her that God was near and was actively watching over her. Despite the human drama that had led her to this point in the wilderness, God was still there as her protector. Hagar's struggle showed her that, despite the challenges she had run from, a future existed for her and her soon-to-be-born son. God revealed Himself anew in this struggle, and Hagar returned for a season to her home. She acted in obedience to God's directive.

Most of us have had similar moments in which we have wrestled with a dilemma and have arrived at a decision that caused us to run away from the madness. We might have felt helpless, alone, and trapped by the circumstances in which we found ourselves. Whether we contributed to the problem or not, whether someone exercised power over us or not, the result is the same: We end up in a wilderness, sitting by a pool hoping for just a moment of relief from the turmoil that is our life, inside and out. And then God shows Himself with all of His glory and power. In that moment, we, like Hagar, come to know who God is, how much He is involved in the details of our lives, and what His Word requires us to do. We are presented with two challenging questions: *Do we recognize God's hand at work in our life? And are we willing to obey Him?*

Do we yield our way to His will, or do we continue to fight our own fight, follow our own plan, or wrestle with a dilemma that is too big for us to handle alone? Struggle takes us into close contact with God. It causes us to speak with God on a new level. It causes us to worship as Hagar did. This obedient response to struggle can be invigorating. It reminds us that God is with us and that He has a plan and a purpose for our experiences. This realization can help us to more fully embrace the idea that all things work toward good, even though the struggle itself may be troubling.

Reflection to Strengthen You for Your Struggle

Do you, like Hagar, see the God who sees you?

What was Hagar's struggle?

What did Hagar's struggle teach her about the nature of God?

What was the impact of Hagar's struggle on her?

What was the impact of Hagar's struggle on others?

How does Hagar's experience with God in this struggle relate to your life?

Jacob: From Struggle to God's Blessing

Genesis 25–33

The story of Jacob and Esau can be seen as a classic case of dysfunctional family dynamics; it's a situation that led to deception and distrust between siblings. These two brothers were radically different men. Esau was a rugged outdoorsman; he loved fishing and hunting. He thrived in that environment and soon became the favorite child of his father, Isaac. Jacob, on the other hand, was more domestic, thriving on those tasks associated with the house. He quickly became his mother's favorite.

Too High a Price

Although Esau was the older son, he was less aware than was Jacob of the cultural value, power, and trappings associated with the firstborn son's position. The oldest son received a double portion of goods from the father and became the head of the family. This was known as the "birthright." In addition, fathers often bestowed additional blessings upon their elder sons. Knowing that Esau valued none of this, Jacob shrewdly took advantage of the situation, agreeing to give Esau the bowl of lentil soup he had asked for—if Esau would give him his birthright. As we see in Genesis 25:29–34, Esau readily agreed to this uneven exchange.

> 29 Once when Jacob was cooking stew, Esau came in from the field, and he was exhausted. 30 And Esau said to Jacob, "Let me eat some of that red stew, for I am exhausted!" (Therefore his name was called Edom.)
> 31 Jacob said, "Sell me your birthright now." 32 Esau said,

"I am about to die; of what use is a birthright to me?"
[33] Jacob said, "Swear to me now." So he swore to him and sold his birthright to Jacob. [34] Then Jacob gave Esau bread and lentil stew, and he ate and drank and rose and went his way. Thus Esau despised his birthright.

I have often thought about this tale. Esau traded his future for a bowl of soup. To us, that may seem ludicrous—*trading away an inheritance for a bowl of soup!* The prize seems unworthy of the price.

That a man would trade his future for momentary physical gratification seems absurd to us today, given our awareness of the value of social capital and power. However, a closer examination of many contemporary decisions reveals that in the quest for momentary physical gratification, men and women in today's culture—accomplished people as well as struggling—regularly make deals similar to Esau's. And those deals often lead to the same disastrous consequences that befell Esau's family. Opting for momentary physical gratification can result in great men losing their positions and the respect of others. Their loving wives and adoring children may suddenly find their family at the center of a media storm that slowly erodes what they thought was the solid bedrock of their world. Eventually a wounded family fades from the public eye.

Conspiracy and Deception

Although Esau had agreed to *give* Jacob his birthright, another deception—years later—was necessary for Jacob to actually *receive* the birthright. Rebekah, the mother of these twins, conspired with Jacob to trick Isaac into bestowing his blessing and the birthright upon Jacob instead of Esau. This final deception enraged Esau so much that he threatened to kill Jacob. Therefore, Rebekah told Jacob to save his life by fleeing to her brother Laban's house.

At his uncle Laban's home, Jacob fell in love with Laban's younger daughter, Rachel, and asked for her hand in marriage. The culture required that Jacob work for his uncle for seven years, after which he would receive his promised bride. Seven years later, on his wedding night, Jacob discovered that he had been tricked into marrying Rachel's older, less attractive sister. Jacob worked for Laban for another seven years in order to earn Rachel's hand.

During his stay with his uncle, Jacob became a shrewd businessman. Laban cheated Jacob, however, and God told Jacob to take Rachel and Leah and his livestock, and return to the land of his father.

Jacob realized that when he reached home he would need to confront a strong and angry older brother. As he traveled, Jacob devised a scheme to appease his brother, because he knew that he and his group would be no match for Esau and his followers. As Jacob and his group got closer to his homeland, Jacob divided his servants and livestock into two groups and sent them ahead of him as gifts for Esau, hoping that this gesture would appease his brother's wrath. Knowing that Esau and his men could easily overpower him, Jacob was afraid. As he drew even closer to home, he received the dire report that Esau was marching toward him with four hundred men at his command.

Blessings from Struggle

The night before he was to ultimately face his brother, Jacob found himself in a physical and emotional struggle. In the past, the conflict between them had been limited to the two brothers themselves, but now Jacob's entire family was at risk as well. We see his prayer in Genesis 32:9–12.

> 9 And Jacob said, "O God of my father Abraham and God of my father Isaac, O Lord who said to me, 'Return to your country and to your kindred, that I may do you good,' 10 I am not worthy of the least of all the deeds of steadfast love and all the faithfulness that you have shown to your servant, for with only my staff I crossed this

Jordan, and now I have become two camps. [11] Please deliver me from the hand of my brother, from the hand of Esau, for I fear him, that he may come and attack me, the mothers with the children [12] But you said, 'I will surely do you good, and make your offspring as the sand of the sea, which cannot be numbered for multitude.'"

Our struggles often lead us to a level of reflection, self-awareness, and confession that will eventually make us stronger in life. Jacob pauses to review what he has gone through, how God has blessed him, his own unworthiness, and his need for deliverance. In other words, Jacob prayed! Jacob was returning in obedience, but he was afraid of what lay ahead. His fear was real, and his concern was not only for himself, but also for the wives and children that God had given him. And then, emotionally exhausted, afraid, and feeling alone, Jacob fell asleep. Genesis 32:24–30 tells us what happened next.

[24] And Jacob was left alone. And a man wrestled with him until the breaking of the day. [25] When the man saw that He did not prevail against Jacob, He touched his hip socket, and Jacob's hip was put out of joint as He wrestled with him. [26] Then He said, "Let me go, for the day has broken." But Jacob said, "I will not let you go unless you bless me." [27] And He said to him, "What is your name?" And he said, "Jacob." [28] Then He said, "Your name shall no longer be called Jacob, but Israel, for you have striven with God and with men, and have prevailed." [29] Then Jacob asked Him, "Please tell me your name." But He said, "Why is it that you ask my name?" And there He blessed him. [30]So Jacob called the name of the place Peniel, saying, "For I have seen God face to face, and yet my life has been delivered."

Jacob, now alone, having sent his wives and children on ahead, had an encounter with God in the form of an angel. Jacob had struggled to be born, struggled to be the heir apparent in his father's house, struggled for position and prestige, struggled to win the woman he loved, struggled to be treated fairly by his uncle, struggled to achieve wealth, and struggled because he did not love one of his wives. Now, on his journey home, alone at last, he is in a position to have the ultimate struggle—with God.

Jacob wrestles all night with the angel, refusing to quit. As morning arrives and he tenaciously holds on, he struggles his way *into a blessing* and an awareness of the future that God has ordained for him. The struggle reveals Jacob's tenacity and assures his blessing. In addition, as a result of the struggle, Jacob's awareness of his own character becomes clearer to him. The angel tells Jacob that he will even have a new name. Jacob had entered the conflict as "Jacob," but he exits as "Israel," which means "struggles with God."

Jacob's struggle changes his life, as God declared a new destiny for him. Yet even as Jacob reels from his injury in the struggle (walking now with a limp as a permanent reminder of his divine encounter), he still seeks to do things his way, to find his own solutions to his problems.

This moment after the blessing is a perfect example of a paradoxical biblical principle known as "already / not yet": God declares some things as already achieved, but people haven't yet experienced them. Even though Jacob had received the angel's blessing, he still arose the next day and developed a scheme to win over his brother's affection—exhibiting the same mindset that he'd had before. Jacob was assuming responsibility for making things right with his offended brother. Even with the blessing of God, he continued to rely on his own wits. He decided to send gifts ahead of his family in hopes of softening his brother's wrath, but God had already provided. In fact, God had provided long ago, when Jacob and Esau were in Rebekah's womb—struggling even then. God let Rebekah know that her older child would serve the younger (Genesis 25:23). So all of Jacob's schemes and deception seem to have been unnecessary.

As Esau and his band of men approached, Esau recognized his brother in the distance and saw him limping. In that moment, Esau's heart was warmed to his brother's plight. While Jacob had been scheming, God had already been moving on the heart of his brother to forgive. What Jacob had assumed would be a battle became an embrace as the brothers were reunited.

Don't miss the principles exhibited here. All of Jacob's struggles contributed to his tenacious character. That character caused him to persevere in his struggle with the angel. The injury that resulted from the struggle became both the quality that worked on his brother Esau's heart and Jacob's constant reminder of God's goodness and of God's promises for Jacob's future.

What injuries are we carrying with us as a result of our struggles? As we look at our injuries, are we mindful of the blessings that came with our victory? Are there moments in our lives that cause us to reflect, meditate, and connect with God? Can we see the blessings that came out of our struggles? If we can pause and look at what God has done in our lives, can see how He has used events to shape our character, and can see how He has taken what could often be viewed as evil and turned it to our good, then we can begin to appreciate the results of our struggles—even the injuries that may have occurred along the way.

Reflection to Strengthen You for Your Struggle
What was Jacob's struggle?
What did Jacob's struggle teach him about the nature of God?
What was the impact of Jacob's struggle on him?
What was the impact of Jacob's struggle on others?

How does Jacob's experience with God in his struggle relate to your life?

Daniel: Standing with Integrity

Daniel 1–6

The powerful story in the sixth chapter of Daniel, including King Darius's eventually sentencing Daniel to the lions' den for praying to God, led to one of the first epiphanies I experienced about the connection between growth, power, and the idea of struggle.

Following God Despite the Risk

Daniel and three of his friends had been taken captive by King Nebuchadnezzar and had been taken to Babylon to be trained to serve in the king's palace. The Babylonians had a unique way of handling captives. Rather than killing all of them, the Babylonians would take the brightest and the best, saturate them with the culture of the empire, remake them in the image of Babylon, and then have them serve the empire.

In Chapter 1, Daniel, Shadrach, Meshach and Abednego are faced with the dilemma of maintain their integrity as Israelites (i.e. following the law of God) or succumbing to the indoctrination of the Babylonians. Daniel and his friends saw submitting to the culture (symbolized by partaking of the food and drink) as defiling themselves. In a bold stand of faith, Daniel said to their guard, "Test your servants for ten days; let us be given vegetables to eat and water to drink. Then let our appearance and the appearance of the youths who eat the king's food be observed by you, and deal with your servants according to what you see. (Daniel 1:12-13). After a vigorous dialogue, the guard reluctantly agreed to this ten day

14

experiment. After ten days, it was obvious that Daniel and his friends were in better shape than any of the other captives.

Don't miss the struggle inherent in this moment. There were many captive Jews, but only these four are recorded as standing on principle, placing their faith in the God they knew, and risking the wrath of a keeper. Whenever someone stands up for a principle, struggle and risk are involved, and often the person's character is also challenged, At the end of the three years' training, the wisdom and understanding of these four men was ten times better than that of the other captives. The four men's willingness to stand up for God made them stand out. God blessed them because of their faithfulness.

Preparing for Future Challenges

Through Bible stories such as Daniel's, God illustrates an important principle: Each struggle invariably prepares us for our *next* challenge, which, if we continue to stand, will be even more of a test at a greater cost. "Next tests" will develop us even further. As Daniel's story shows us, "next challenges" will often be multi-pronged and will involve greater personal learning if we endure and greater glory to God in the eyes of others!

We might think that the four captives, having successfully entered the Babylonian world, would have smooth sailing. However, life is more complex than that. The men's principles once again placed them in conflict with the ruling powers. The king, fully convinced of his own godhood, instituted a public decree that all should bow to his image when the horns sounded. Any disobedience would result in death.

When the horns sounded, the people bowed. However, Shadrach, Meshach, and Abednego stood. Their enemies quickly reported their disobedience to the king. The three men were dragged before the king and were confronted with the charges against them.

Their response, recorded in Daniel 3:16-18, is a classic example of taking a stand on principle in the midst of struggle.

> [16] Shadrach, Meshach, and Abednego answered and said to the king, "O Nebuchadnezzar, we have no need to answer you in this matter. [17] If this be so, our God whom we serve is able to deliver us from the burning fiery furnace, and He will deliver us out of your hand, O king. [18] But if not, be it known to you, O king, that we will not serve your gods or worship the golden image that you have set up."

Their response was clear. They were basically saying, "We will not bow. Our Lord can deliver us, but even if He chooses not to, we will not bow!" This is what author Linda Tobey would call "decision in the moment of integrity."[1] Adversity and struggle help to reveal our level of faith and our level of commitment in the face of danger, in the midst of struggle. By taking this stand, the men left the king only one option—to condemn them to death in the fiery furnace. We don't know whether they went into the fire without fear. However, we *do* know that they went into this perilous situation with their faith unyielding!

Daniel 3:19 tells us that the fire was heated "seven times hotter" than it is usually heated, killing those who threw the men into that inferno. Surely this would be certain death for the three Israelites! The men's enemies breathed a sigh of relief. But as the king watched, he suddenly realized that the three men were now four! Rather than seeing the men perish, he saw them standing strong, standing well protected in the middle of the raging fire— thriving in the midst of the struggle! King Nebuchadnezzar saw the presence of God manifested in the furnace and consequently in the men's lives, in their stand, in their ultimate faith in their God. Their stand in the struggle caused even this pagan king to declare, "There is no other God who is able to rescue in this way" (Daniel 3:29).

The Fruit of Integrity

Intense struggle is always fraught with the chance of destruction—at least when looking with a natural eye, rather than with a spiritual one. What would the three men have gained had they bowed to the pressure to compromise their principles? Likely another day of life, but at what cost to their integrity and to their walk of faith? What would have been the testimony of the king had they bowed? How else could God have been magnified had they not taken a stand based upon their faith? The impact of their stand was the glorification of God, their deepened understanding of God, and an experience that solidified their belief in truths that Paul would later write in Philippians: "My God will supply every need of yours according to His riches in glory in Christ Jesus" (4:19), and "I can do all things through Him [Christ] who strengthens me!" (4:13).

Severe struggle causes us to recall what God said to Joshua in Joshua 1:9—"Have I not commanded you? Be strong and courageous. Do not be frightened, and do not be dismayed, for the LORD your God is with you wherever you go."

The intensity of our struggle causes us to pull from deep within us the admonition found in Proverbs 3:5–6.

> 5 Trust in the Lord with all your heart, and do not
> lean on your own understanding. 6 In all your ways
> acknowledge Him, and He will make straight your paths.

Daniel's Character and Integrity

As we continue reading the saga of Daniel recounted in Chapter 6, we see the level of respect, trust, and admiration that Daniel enjoyed. He had become one of three overseers of 120 governors, and even with that degree of responsibility he continued to perform at such a high level of excellence that the king contemplated elevating him to a position over the whole kingdom.

This favor of the king was not lost upon Daniel's two colleagues and the leaders they supervised. They wanted to diminish Daniel's standing in the king's eyes. They were aware, however, that they could not attack the character of Daniel. His lifestyle was above reproach. He walked his faith! He lived his faith! He exemplified the principles of his faith. He still stood with the same integrity that had caused him to refuse to partake of the king's table when he was first captured. So Daniel's colleagues and their team hatched a plot that would pit political power against Daniel and his faith. This plot is described in Daniel 6:4–10, below.

> [4] Then the high officials and the satraps sought to find a ground for complaint against Daniel with regard to the kingdom, but they could find no ground for complaint or any fault, because he was faithful, and no error or fault was found in him. [5] Then these men said, "We shall not find any ground for complaint against this Daniel unless we find it in connection with the law of his God."
>
> [6] Then these high officials and satraps came by agreement to the king and said to him, "O King Darius, live forever! [7] All the high officials of the kingdom, the prefects and the satraps, the counselors and the governors are agreed that the king should establish an ordinance and enforce an injunction, that whoever makes petition to any god or man for thirty days, except to you, O king, shall be cast into the den of lions. [8] Now, O king, establish the injunction and sign the document, so that it cannot be changed, according to the law of the Medes and the Persians, which cannot be revoked." [9] Therefore King Darius signed the document and injunction.

Very deliberately, without breaking stride, Daniel went through his daily prayer regimen, knowing that this action could cost him his life.

¹⁰ When Daniel knew that the document had been signed, he went to his house where he had windows in his upper chamber open toward Jerusalem. He got down on his knees three times a day and prayed and gave thanks before his God, as he had done previously.

Of course, Daniel knew how the king would respond. Daniel was not a novice. He had been an integral part of the king's court for a long time. He understood the politics. He understood the culture. Yet he embraced the risk. He embraced the struggle that was to come. Embracing means looking into the face of the critical choice or the critical enemy or the critical circumstance before you—and leaning into it. In such situations, you cannot afford a backward glance. Such moments give us a crystal-clear picture of who we are, and we can be awed when we see what God is able to do on our behalf.

Daniel's Testimony

Daniel had to determine who he was within his heart, just as he and his colleagues had done in Daniel 1. When Daniel resolved not to defile himself, he had made a decision to be consistent in his principles—in other words, he had decided to behave in alignment with his beliefs. Struggle refines us, purifies us, clarifies within us what we will live for—and what we are willing to die for.

After Daniel had been put into the lions' den, King Darius arrived the next morning—eagerly, desperately wanting to see if Daniel was alive. He joyfully found Daniel standing, unharmed despite the king's own ruling. Daniel was able to boldly say, "O king, live forever! My God sent His angel and shut the lions' mouths, and they have not harmed me, because I was found blameless before Him; and also before you, O king, I have done no harm" (Daniel 6:21–22). Daniel's struggle impacted not just himself, but all who were a part of this event!

Look at the power of Daniel's testimony. Despite what could have happened and what *should* have happened under natural circumstances, Daniel had survived! Despite the desire of Daniel's enemies and a well thought out plan to discredit him and take his life, Daniel was still standing!

"My God sent His angel and shut the lions' mouths!" Daniel could look at his situation and boldly declare that the object of his faith—the God he trusted—had taken care of him, and had assured him through this deliverance that He was able and willing to sustain him during a dangerous situation. Daniel's God was a God of the supernatural. By becoming involved in Daniel's personal dilemma God had shown Daniel and others the power that He would exercise time and time again. He could override the laws of nature, and He was always in ultimate control of every situation.

"I was found blameless before Him [God]." Daniel had shown himself to be innocent of a weak faith. Yet who could have blamed him if he had succumbed to the pressures to yield to the king's demand and had ceased to pray to God? Who could have faulted him for renouncing God as he was about to be thrown into the lions' den? We all want to live, but at what costs to our character, and to our testimony to a world that desperately seeks some semblance of sustained integrity? Daniel was found innocent of wrongdoing before God and before man.

Daniel's actions and his testimony had a profound effect on King Darius—and consequently on many others. After Daniel's night in the lions' den, Daniel 6:25–26a tells us, "Then King Darius wrote to all the peoples, nations, and languages that dwell in all the earth: 'Peace be multiplied to you. I make a decree, that in all my royal dominion people are to tremble and fear before the God of Daniel." As a result of God's deliverance of Daniel, King Darius was so impacted that he declared that the God of Daniel would be revered throughout the kingdom.

The Impact of Daniel's Integrity on Others

It's fair to ask, "Why would God allow Daniel to be faced with the struggles chronicled in Daniel 6? Couldn't God simply have used Daniel and the skills that were placed in him to do the work that God laid out before him?" Of course, the answer is Yes, God could have done that. However, it's important to see the broader picture, to look beyond Daniel and to consider the impact that Daniel's struggle had on others. Let's examine the people one at a time.

First, King Darius: In order to confront his own vanity, the king was made to realize that his egocentric ruling had compelled him to condemn a just man to death. The situation caused him anguish, a struggle with his own conscience, and a night's rest.

Second, the other governors and rulers: They were exposed for who they were—a manipulative crew whose only strength was their self-promotion. Rather than becoming aware of their own character flaws, they yielded to the kind of thinking and actions that come from jealous hearts. In the end, Daniel's struggles cost them their lives. His stand exposed their character and their motives.

What might have been the impact of Daniel's stand on his own people who knew him? What do you suppose went through their minds as they heard the decrees and resigned themselves to indulging the whims of those in power because they wanted to live (not a terrible motivation at all!)? Yet news of Daniel's stand must have reached them.

As we reflect upon these questions, we might think of Paul several centuries later, sentenced to prison for preaching the gospel. He wrote from jail and testified of the joy that he felt, even while imprisoned, because he heard that the gospel was being preached with even more boldness, for all kinds of reasons. Some people were preaching because they were encouraged by Paul's own stand, while others were preaching because they hoped to cause Paul even more anguish from his captors.

Paul was so committed to the virtues of struggle that he could boldly state the following: "In every way, whether in pretense or in truth, Christ is proclaimed, and in that I rejoice" (Philippians 1:18). I can imagine that Daniel, too, was aware that others would benefit from his struggle—or, if he did *not* take a stand, would weaken in their own commitment. Our struggles matter to others! Our struggles are not ours alone!

An Example of Integrity from Recent Times

Nelson Mandela of South Africa, who led the struggle to end apartheid there, is an example of a principled person from more recent times. As an attorney, Mandela, along with his colleagues, took case after case to the courts as they sought to dismantle a racist system that made a majority of the indigenous people of the land second-class citizens. Mandela was eventually thrown into prison.

As the years passed, he was given opportunity after opportunity to gain his freedom. All he'd need to do was to denounce his organization that was committed to ending apartheid; then he would be free to walk the streets again—still in the same culture, still with the same injustices, but free of the four walls of his cell. Mandela would not denounce his organization. His stand cost him years with his family, years of his health, years of his profession. In fact, it cost him twenty-seven years of his life, and it cost him his marriage. Yet Mandela stood firm on principle. When he was finally released from prison, he was able to become the moral voice of his nation. He left prison, not with a desire to punish his jailers, but with a desire to build a nation that would be a united South Africa.

Strengthening Our Own Integrity

Ardent struggle can purify us, cleanse us of the hypocrisies in our own life, help us to realize what we truly believe, and show us what God can accomplish through us.

One of the adversities that Daniel faced was the envy of others. It's important to recognize that Daniel had no control over that. Human nature and people's responses to us are totally out of our control if their rejection of us is based upon their own issues.

Ultimately Paul's declaration in Romans 8:38–39 speaks to our dilemma in our struggles: "I am sure that neither death nor life, nor angels nor rulers, nor things present nor things to come, nor powers, [39] nor height nor depth, nor anything else in all creation, will be able to separate us from the love of God in Christ Jesus our Lord." We must have this same attitude if we are to face personalized hatred, unjust laws, and the natural predators of this life!

I ask myself, "Am I able, am I willing to take such a stand? Am I willing to stand as Daniel stood, without compromise, without breaking stride in living out the principles of my faith? Am I able to face the consequences, to go through what could be a life-and-death struggle solely for my principles? What do I risk if I choose to embrace struggle? But more important, what do I risk if I *fail* to embrace struggle? What would happen to my own growth? What would happen to the opportunities for others to witness the power of God in my life as I face my struggles?"

Reflection to Strengthen You for Your Struggle
What were Daniel's struggles?
What did Daniel's struggles teach him about the nature of God?
What was the impact of Daniel's struggle on him?
What was the impact of Daniel's struggle on others?
How does Daniel's experience with God in his struggles relate to your life?

Tobey, Linda. "The Integrity Moment." | January 28, 2005, https://www.masoncontractors.org/2005/01/28/the-integrity-moment/#newsletter

David: Facing Giants

1 Samuel 16–17

The story of David and Goliath is one of those amazing narratives that reads like a great adventure tale. Many of us grew up with the image of the little boy dramatically killing the giant with a single stone from his slingshot. We marvel at David's courage, especially when other more experienced warriors were terrified of Goliath and reluctant to accept his challenge.

Prepared for Battle

The struggles that David had faced before he met Goliath on the battlefield had prepared him in several ways for this pivotal moment—a moment that elevated him to the equivalent of a pop culture hero in the eyes of the people.

David's illustrious journey to a battlefield victory over a giant who had made an entire army fearful began with David serving as a shepherd of his father's flocks. The background seems to indicate that as the youngest son David was thought of literally as the little brother of no consequence. The prophet Samuel describes how God had directed him to the house of Jesse with the instruction that one of Jesse's sons should be anointed as the next king of Israel.

The story is a familiar one: Jesse presents seven of his sons to Samuel, but none of them is the one God has chosen. Then Samuel asks, "Is there another?" When David, who has been tending his father's sheep, is presented, the LORD immediately identifies him as the one He has chosen to be the next king of Israel, and Samuel anoints him.

What happened next? Not what you might expect. There was no parade, no confrontation with the current king, no coronation, no revolution. Instead, *David returned to tending the sheep.*

Years passed—one of the greatest periods of meditation and preparation that a man could have. David had time to spend learning how to be a loving, protective, bold, and daring shepherd. He had the opportunity to fight both a bear and a lion in defense of his sheep. And he was victorious on each occasion. He had a chance to consider how the relationship between him and his flock of sheep mirrored the relationship between God and His people. David learned to act courageously in defense of those who could not defend themselves.

Even with all of that reflection, it seems likely that a young man who had been told that he would become the next king sometimes wondered when that—or when *something*—would happen. He might have wondered whether Samuel's proclamation would ever become reality. After all, nothing changed for David after his anointing.

Waiting: My Personal Struggle

I can identify with the struggle of waiting. I have occasionally heard the voice of God speaking in my spirit, challenging me to next levels while I continued to be faithful where I was planted at the time. I always had dreams of more, of doing something truly meaningful, something that would be significant for others as well as for myself. I dreamed of standing before audiences sharing, teaching, motivating, creating, and leading. Yet often I simply needed to quiet my spirit while I learned the lessons that God had for me at that time. Although I yearned for a larger challenge, these times of waiting are their own unique struggle; it can be difficult to be faithful over the few things while watching others engage the many. Yet even these moments yield fruit.

Even before his encounter with Goliath, David was described in 1 Samuel 16:18b as "a man of valor, a man of war, prudent in speech . . . *and the* LORD *is with him.*" These are the attributes of a king, a visionary leader, and a good shepherd who can both lead and defend. These traits were nurtured during David's long wait, during his many encounters with beasts that could harm his sheep.

The Battle Itself

One fateful day, David ventured to the frontline of the war to see his brothers, now part of the army of Israelites that was battling the Philistines. He hears Goliath boldly and callously challenging the Jews to send out their greatest champion to fight him, winner take all. While Saul and his army stand in awe of this giant, David's only thought is "Who is this uncircumcised Philistine, that he should defy the armies of the living God?" (1 Samuel 17:26). An epic struggle follows, as David steps forward to fight Goliath—not with traditional armor, not with any human backup, but with the same tools he has used successfully before.

By considering how this battle unfolded, we can find much to apply to our own situation. First, we must know our own strengths. We must gauge what will work for us and what will not. We must understand that what works for others may not work well for us as we face challenges.

David was urged to put on Saul's armor. While the suggestion seemed very practical, another man's armor was not a good fit for David. In the end, David went into this struggle with the same faith and literally with the same weapons he had used as a shepherd. He carried with him a sling and five stones, and he also carried an awareness of who would ultimately be the source of his victory— God Himself.

David was well acquainted with the power of God, as each of us must be if we are to rely on Him in our struggles. Knowing God, remembering His deliverance of us in the past, and recognizing His ability to deliver us again and again, should impact how we choose to face the giants at the center of the struggles in our life.

David rushed toward the giant—faith in his heart, courage in his spirit, and sling in his hand. David charged toward Goliath, *going at him*, declaring to Goliath that this would be the day that he would be delivered into David's hands! The words from 1 Samuel 17:45–51 tell the story most effectively:

> [45] Then David said to the Philistine, "You come to me with a sword and with a spear and with a javelin, but I come to you in the name of the Lord of hosts, the God of the armies of Israel, whom you have defied. [46] This day the Lord will deliver you into my hand, and I will strike you down and cut off your head. And I will give the dead bodies of the host of the Philistines this day to the birds of the air and to the wild beasts of the earth, that all the earth may know that there is a God in Israel, [47] and that all this assembly shall know that the Lord saves not with sword and spear. For the battle is the Lord's, and He will give you into our hand."
>
> [48] When the Philistine arose and came and drew near to meet David, David ran quickly toward the battle line to meet the Philistine. [49] And David put his hand in his bag and took out a stone and slung it and struck the Philistine on his forehead. The stone sank into his forehead, and he fell on his face to the ground. [50] So David prevailed over the Philistine with a sling and with a stone, and struck the Philistine and killed him. There was no sword in the hand of David. [51] Then David ran and stood over the Philistine and took his sword and drew it out of its sheath and killed him and cut off his head with it. When the Philistines saw that their champion was dead, they fled.

Learning from David's Struggle

David's earlier encounters with adversity had prepared him spiritually, mentally, emotionally, spiritually, and physically to face this giant with faith, not with fear. His earlier struggles had prepared him to attempt what others feared to even consider—facing a giant despite the appearance of danger.

Scripture is replete with teachings about faith, but experiences (such as fighting giants) make the abstract tangible. David's face-off with Goliath reminds us of some characteristics of the giants that we face in our own lives. Goliath (the giant) was real, not a figment of David's imagination. Goliath was strong, and he was vicious. To have treated him as anything else could have gotten David killed.

Closer scrutiny reveals the following important points about *our* struggles (symbolized by Goliath).

Goliath is not always what he seems to be. He may appear to be invincible. You may seem to be alone when facing him. You may feel outnumbered, even helpless. But you need to consider the situation from God's perspective: "No weapon that is fashioned against you shall succeed" (Isaiah 54:17a), and "[You] can do all things through Him [Christ] who strengthens [you]" (Philippians 4:13).

Goliath (the struggle) has a divine purpose in your life. David's experience fighting Goliath allowed David to demonstrate courage through faith. It allowed David to once again experience the power of God in his life.

Goliath is no match for God. Goliath is big to be sure. And your giant is daunting, But God is so much bigger! Your struggle with your giant reveals the full nature of God. God is all-powerful. He is a covenant-keeper. He is a protector.

Goliath (our struggle) presents us with the opportunity to experience God at new levels. These struggles and conflicts inform our awareness of who God is and the power He has to protect us when we face unimaginable odds.

Goliaths make our faith more tangible. In Philippians 4:19, one of his later writings, Paul boldly proclaims, "My God will supply every need of yours according to His riches in glory in Christ Jesus." In

28

order for Paul to have been so bold in that declaration, he must have had some experience with God meeting his needs. Living through struggle produces this kind of boldness. Wrestling with the unimaginable causes this kind of clarity.

Our struggles also produce confidence and trust—confidence in the power of God to deliver, and trust to accept God's will for us if He chooses *not* to deliver.

As we have seen, we benefit from our struggles in many ways. However, the benefits of our struggles are never exclusively for us as individuals. Because God has a plan, we must begin to see our role in His plan, to see God using our lives as instruction for others.

Reflection to Strengthen You for Your Struggle
What was David's struggle?
What did David's struggle teach him about the nature of God?
What was the impact of David's struggle on him?
What was the impact of David's struggle on others?
How does David's experience with God in his struggle relate to your life?

Jonah: Repentance and Praise in Struggle

Jonah 1–4

Sometimes God allows defeats to occur within our struggles. However, He uses those defeats to teach us more about Him. The Israelites of Scripture were occasionally defeated in battles and were led into various captivities as a result of their disobedience to God and their rejection of God's principles. Sometimes our struggles, like those of the Israelites, are a natural consequence of our own decisions. In those cases, we likely have something to learn, and our struggle results in personal growth. We may be the ones who benefit most from our struggle, but others may benefit as well.

God's Command—and Jonah's Response

Such was the case with Jonah, a minor prophet to whom God gave an assignment: "Arise, go to Nineveh, that great city, and call out against it, for their evil has come up before me" (Jonah 1:2). There was no ambiguity in God's command to Jonah. Jonah was told to get up, was told where to go, and finally was told what to do when he arrived at his destination. He was even told why he was going. The Ninevites were no mystery to Jonah; he knew them well—so well that he despised them!

The Ninevites were a brutal people with a history of torturing their captives. Their historical abuse of the Israelites and others was well known to Jonah. So when Jonah received his command from God, he got up—but rather than going to Nineveh, he fled in the opposite direction, choosing to go instead to Tarshish. Jonah ran from the will of God! He sought to escape from the presence of the

LORD. This is an amazing decision for a prophet to make. For a prophet—one who has spent time with God, has communicated with God, and has experienced the power and presence of God—to seek to escape God's presence seems ludicrous. However, *we* make similar decisions daily, as we seek to live out our own agendas in life, rather than do that which we know is right or that which we know God is calling us to do.

Once Jonah is aboard the ship to Tarshish, he settles in for his journey—an intentional journey away from Nineveh and away from the will of God. However, the Scriptures demonstrate that God is not content to leave us in our disobedience. This short narrative illustrates a key attribute of God—He will intervene to be sure that we become aware of our own folly and that we ultimately fulfill the mission He has designed for us. *He will become actively involved in people's lives.*

Jonah's first struggle was in yielding his own agenda to the will of God. He allowed his own disdain (some say *fear*) of the Ninevites to prevent him from being obedient to God's will. How often do we face this in our lives? For a variety of reasons, we often choose to do the opposite of what God is clearly saying to us in His written Word, or we deliberately ignore the directives that His Spirit is impressing upon our own lives. How often have we found ourselves in a downward spiral similar to Jonah's?

At Sea

A storm rages on the sea. The sailors—very experienced seafarers—find themselves struggling in a life-threatening situation, throwing everything overboard in a desperate attempt to save their own lives as well as the life of their passenger. The situation becomes so dire that they eventually awaken Jonah, who quickly recognizes that his disobedience is the cause of their dilemma. Jonah's acknowledgment of his responsibility for their difficulty becomes the first benefit of his struggle. Jonah confesses his own disobedience. Confession is critical to beginning the transition from struggle to growth—for Jonah and for us. Confession frees people to develop, and to advance to higher levels.

In Psalm 32:3–4, David (the subject of the previous chapter in this book) described the internal turmoil that accompanies disobedience and unrepented sin. When he kept silent about his sin, his bones wasted away through his day-long groaning. He felt God's heavy hand upon him day and night. His vitality withered.

This mighty king was being overwhelmed by his own internal struggle, because he had neglected to confess his internal sin. When David later acknowledged his sin and confessed his own rebelliousness, God heard him and forgave him. David's relationship with God and his vitality were restored.

Once Jonah, like David, acknowledges his sin, he is free to begin his period of learning and growth. Meanwhile the sailors are still faced with the very real danger of a sinking ship. While disposing of Jonah is the most obvious answer, they are reluctant to do that and valiantly begin to throw everything else overboard. Finally, reality sets in. Though the sailors agonize over taking a life, they throw Jonah overboard at his own insistence. Immediately a "great fish" swallows him. When Jonah went into the water, he expected to die for his disobedience. However, in reality, his time in the water becomes yet another struggle on his journey toward renewal and toward the completion of his mission.

Reflecting on Jonah's Actions

It's easy to see Jonah's situation as punishment for his disobedience, for the foolishness he demonstrated in his effort to run from God. However, I challenge you with another perspective: that the fish swallowing Jonah was actually an act of grace!

You may be thinking, "How can spending time in this nightmare scenario be an 'act of grace'? How can being caught in the belly of a fish be an act of grace?" To answer these questions, we must first consider the natural consequence that Jonah anticipated when he volunteered to be thrown overboard: *He expected to die!* He expected his life to end in disgrace after his disobedience! The sea was raging; Jonah was in the natural elements with no hope of survival. *Yet he lived!* This is grace.

How can the turmoil you are currently wrestling with—turmoil that you know is a direct result of your own decision-making—be an act of grace? This is true for you just as it was for Jonah: You are still alive! You are still here! You have been given an opportunity, you have been given time, during this season in your life, to do three things: *to repent, to reaffirm* your core beliefs, and *to reconnect* with God.

Let's notice what Jonah did when he found himself in an unexpected predicament that resulted mainly from his own disobedience. Chapter 2 begins with Jonah's prayer praising God. He is still in the belly of the fish, still very much in the middle of his dilemma. He acknowledges his precarious situation, calling it the belly of hell. We have likely experienced that feeling at one time or another—at a time when life's challenges seemed overwhelming. Jonah praises God for hearing him, even as he is tightly tangled in seaweed, choking from his circumstances. Jonah does not sugarcoat his dilemma; rather he praises God anyway. He expresses a desire for renewed relationship. He refocuses on what is most important to him—the relationship he sought to escape! Jonah recommits to God in these moments. He testifies that true salvation is found only in God.

Jonah's forced isolation and immediate peril brought clarity to his perspective. Amazingly, miraculously, providentially the fish throws Jonah onto dry land, where God repeats his instruction: "Go to Nineveh to preach!" In essence, Jonah is repositioned to be obedient, repositioned to serve, repositioned to refocus on the task at hand. This is Jonah's second chance. God gives second chances, new beginnings. This is an important attribute to recognize about God: Our life circumstances are fatal only if God says they are.

I call these monumental struggles in our lives "belly-of-the-fish moments"—times when we find ourselves in dire circumstances as a result of our own decisions and/or actions. Our behavior in these moments has a critical impact on the next steps in our lives. These seasons in life may be short or they may be long, depending upon our learning curve and upon the lessons God has for us. Jonah was in this great fish for three days; then he was released to complete his mission. The Israelites were in the wilderness for forty years, but they wouldn't have needed forty years to cover the distance they traveled. They had some maturing to do, some attitudes to change. They needed to become a people who had a close relationship with God, who could face military enemies, and who could possess the land that God had promised them.

Completing His Mission

When Jonah reached Nineveh—now focused and passionate about obedience—he preached a simple yet powerful message to his former enemy: *"Repent!"* And the Ninevites heard his message! The people heard the preached word and repented. The king heard about this movement among the people and followed suit. Although Jonah still has frustrations—and God continues to work with him—the record clearly shows that Jonah's experience with the great fish helped him to better understand the nature of God and the necessity of obedience to God.

Jonah's struggle actually prepared him to take on the mission that lay before him—to preach to a people he hated, to present the message of salvation to a people whom he really wanted God to punish. Jonah not only preached; he preached with great power and conviction! People were saved as a result of his preaching. I can imagine the impact of this man—haggard and smelly, with skin bleached from the belly of the fish—boldly proclaiming the judgment of God on his enemy, and describing the mercy God offered for their repentance of their sinful state.

Aftermath

The Ninevites repented after hearing Jonah's message. God accepted them just as Jonah knew He would. Yet Jonah's struggle continued as he wrestled with his own personal issues. This small book of the Old Testament does not tell us how Jonah resolved his own internal struggles. Further reading in Chapter 4 reveals that Jonah was still filled with bitterness about the salvation of the Ninevites—so much so that he literally says to God, "Take my life!" at least twice in that final chapter.

Ultimately Jonah's struggle was an internal one. His act of apparent obedience— effectively presenting the message of repentance to a lost nation—failed to penetrate his own heart. Sometimes issues that we perceive to be about others are really about ourselves. And sometimes issues that we perceive to be external battles are, in reality, internal battles—and those struggles are often the most frustrating.

Jonah's story highlights for us the proper response whenever we find ourselves in desolate, precarious circumstances that result from our own disobedience. In those times of struggle, we must remember to pray and praise, repent, reaffirm our core beliefs, and reconnect with the God who knows and loves us, and gives us the grace to live another day.

Jonah's three days, or the Israelites' forty years—which track are you on? Are you using your struggle to pray to God, to praise Him for the grace He has extended to you? Are you embracing the truth that Paul shared in Romans 8:28b—"For those who love God all things work together for the good, for those who are called according to His purpose"? Are you taking advantage of the grace that you have been given to reconnect with God?

Reflection to Strengthen You for Your Struggle

What was Jonah's struggle?

What did Jonah's struggle teach him about the nature of God?

What was the impact of Jonah's struggle on him?

What was the impact of Jonah's struggle on others?

How does Jonah's experience with God in his struggle relate to your life?

Joseph: Blessed in the Land of His Affliction

Genesis 37, 39, 41

Let's take a moment and listen in on a moment of praise from Joseph, the youngest son of Israel (Jacob from the second chapter of this book). This moment is found in Genesis 41:46–52. It's easy to imagine Joseph standing in a window, looking out over land in Egypt, a hand on a shoulder of each of his small sons as he pauses and savors this moment.

> 46 Joseph was thirty years old when he entered the service of Pharaoh king of Egypt. And Joseph went out from the presence of Pharaoh and went through all the land of Egypt. 47 During the seven plentiful years the earth produced abundantly, 48 and he gathered up all the food of these seven years, which occurred in the land of Egypt, and put the food in the cities. He put in every city the food from the fields around it. 49 And Joseph stored up grain in great abundance, like the sand of the sea, until he ceased to measure it, for it could not be measured. 50 Before the year of famine came, two sons were born to Joseph. Asenath, the daughter of Potiphera priest of On, bore them to him. 51 Joseph called the name of the firstborn Manasseh. "For," he said, "God has made me forget all my hardship and all my father's house." 52 The name of the second he called Ephraim, "For God has made me fruitful in the land of my affliction."

These verses reflect a triumphant moment for Joseph, but they do not reflect his journey of challenge and turmoil that had preceded this moment. To really appreciate this moment in which Joseph implements a master plan designed to preserve Egypt and his own people during a devastating famine, we must consider the amazing story that had led him to this point.

With His Brothers

Joseph was the youngest of twelve sons. He was victimized by his brothers, who grew weary of the obvious favor their father showed him and grew angry at Joseph's visions of one day ruling over them. As Joseph approached them one day on an errand from their father, they hatched a plot to dispose of him once and for all. They easily overpowered Joseph, stripped him of his coat of many colors (a symbol of his father's favor), and threw him into a waterless pit to die.

As God would have it, the plot shifted, and Joseph was instead sold to a caravan of people on their way to Egypt. The favored Joseph had become a slave. What challenges he had to overcome over the next thirteen years to prepare him for the moment we read about at the beginning of this chapter!

Joseph had been terrified in the deep, dark pit that his brothers had thrown him into, and he had surely expected that he would die. His pleas for mercy had been drowned out by the sound of laughter, drinking, and celebration of his brothers. How could Joseph reconcile his current situation with the visions that God had given him for his future and the future of his family? In that moment alone, Joseph's emotional turmoil would seem to have been unbearable.

Our challenges do that to us—they confront us with realities that do not align with our hopes. Our challenges stand as contradictions to all of the promises that we believe God has given us—all of the assurances we have come to accept as truth. Joseph must have had to muster his reserves of faith and courage to stay focused on the God he believed in and served. And at the height of

39

Joseph's despair, things had gotten even worse: Joseph had been hoisted from the pit, sold into slavery, and dragged from his homeland to an unknown future in an unknown land.

Head of His Master's Household

In time, Joseph became the leader of his master's household, handling all of his master's business, overseeing all of the affairs of the house—and performing with excellence! He was still a slave, but serving as a slave in the home of a leading citizen—with that citizen's full authority and trust—was a far cry from the dark pit to which Joseph had been sentenced.

Then Joseph encountered a new kind of challenge—not a life-or-death challenge like the pit, but a challenge fraught with danger nevertheless: The wife of Joseph's master began to pursue Joseph with a level of intensity that caused him to avoid her presence, which only further attracted her.

While Joseph had been in the pit, he'd had no choices regarding his survival. He simply needed to trust God. If Joseph didn't know it before, he learned in that pit that God was the ultimate source of his deliverance—that the God who gave him dreams would preserve him until those dreams became reality. Surely that is an "Aha! moment" for many of us in times of challenge—recognizing that we have no option but to trust the God who declares in His Word that "I will not leave you or forsake you" (Joshua 1:5b). In the middle of a moral dilemma, Joseph *had* to make a decision about how to avoid sinning against God and abusing the trust of his master. And Joseph chose to *run*!

In Prison

How frustrating it is to do the right thing and still be accused, convicted, and sentenced by those who have the power to impact our life! Joseph finds himself imprisoned, based on a lie told by his master's wife. This reminds us that we can be right, we can be true, we can act with integrity, and we can still find ourselves unjustly accused and imprisoned—perhaps for decades. Joseph enters this new arena with his integrity and faith intact, however, and even within a prison he once again rises to the height of power.

The scene at the beginning of this chapter, with Joseph celebrating all that God had done for him in the land of his affliction, took place *after* Joseph's time in prison, so we know that Joseph overcame his adversities. To read even *beyond* that point of Joseph's story—to an even sweeter ending—read Genesis, Chapters 42–47.

Growing Through Challenges

Let's look more closely at the challenges Joseph faced and how they impacted his growth and his eventual position of power in Egypt. We often hear the principle stated in Luke 12:48b—"Everyone to whom much was given, of him much will be required," meaning that those of us who have been given great gifts and positions of influence must take on greater responsibilities in our lives, in society. But Joseph's story gives us something else to consider in relation to this principle.

Notice the pattern in the challenges Joseph faced: Joseph entered a pit and exited a slave. He became a lead slave in Potiphar's house and exited a prisoner. As an inmate, he was put in charge of all of the prisoners and eventually, after he was released from prison, became second in command of the entire nation of Egypt. Each challenge—which came upon Joseph as a result of his mistreatment by others—eventually took him to a new level of responsibility. Surely this isn't the path that Joseph would have chosen to prepare himself to be the leader that God's vision had already declared! Who would choose jail? Who would choose slavery? Who would choose such a path? Yet it is the journey ordained by God. Joseph learned a number of lessons on his journey:

- He had to trust in God with all that was in him.

41

- He had to walk in integrity—no matter what was going on around him, no matter where he was or what others did.
- God was able to protect him and help him in moments of struggle.
- God had a plan for his life and would fulfill His declared promise.
- God would supply all of his needs.
- No situation is too hard for God.
- God's timing was not *his* timing, but God's plan would come to pass at the perfect time.
- No matter his circumstances, he was on a continuous journey with God, who was molding and shaping him into the man God had ordained him to be.

Looking Forward

At the pinnacle of his power in Egypt, Joseph says, "God has made me forget all my hardship and all my father's house" (Genesis 41:51b). Joseph is expressing the same sentiment that Paul will later write in Philippians 3:13b–14: "Forgetting what lies behind and straining forward to what lies ahead, I press on toward the goal for the prize of the upward call of God in Christ Jesus."

Joseph sees God as the source of his ability to avoid being caught up in the trauma of the past—to forget it *all*, both the envy of his brothers in his father's house and the toil he suffered first as a slave and then as a prisoner. Joseph forgot the fighting, the ridicule, the treachery, the hatred; the slavery, the lies told about him, the loss of faith in him, and the long imprisonment for a crime he did not commit.

Not only did God cause Joseph to forget these sorrowful experiences, He blessed Joseph with children and power in the very place that he had suffered indignity after indignity. Joseph went from slave to prisoner to prime minister over a thirteen-year period.

And all of that happened so that Joseph might fulfill God's plan for His people.

As you pause to reflect upon your own struggles in life, are you able to let go of the painful past that may exist? Can you embrace the possible challenges of the present and be excited about God's promises for your future? Can you see God's hand on your life even when you were embroiled in conflict or faced with the consequences of personal betrayal?

Joseph's story encourages us to embrace God's current challenges as well as His current blessings, to learn from our past, and to consider how our past prepared us for the responsibilities God may have planned for our future.

Reflection to Strengthen You for Your Struggle
What were Joseph's struggles?
What did Joseph's struggles teach him about the nature of God?
What was the impact of Joseph's struggles on him?
What was the impact of Joseph's struggles on others?
How does Joseph's experience with God in his struggles relate to your life?

Esther: Struggling to Accept God's Call

Esther 1–9

Esther was a beautiful young woman who was catapulted into the position of Queen of Persia. Like Joseph in the previous chapter of this book, Esther found herself with an unexpected opportunity to save her people.

Positioned for a Purpose

Esther's circumstances ultimately brought her to realize who she was and what her purpose was in life. God is not a God of chance or coincidence. Each of us can know that our lives have purpose—that there was intentionality to our creation. As God said to Jeremiah in Jeremiah 1:5,

> Before I formed you in the womb I knew you, and
> before you were born I consecrated you; I appointed you a
> prophet to the nations.

Circumstances fraught with struggle and moments of decision confirmed for Esther who she really was—as a woman and as a Jew.

After the King of Persia had invited young women of the land to appear at the palace so that he might select one of them as his new queen, Mordecai, Esther's uncle and guardian—and a Jew in Persia—encouraged Esther to enter the competition. Esther's natural beauty immediately caught the king's eye, and she was selected, along with several other young women, to go through a year of preparation before the king would formally select one of them as his new wife and queen.

Haman's Trick

Esther's story involves not only romance but also intrigue, as a subplot develops involving Mordecai, whom Haman, one of the king's cabinet members, had grown to dislike. Mordecai, on the other hand, does not trust the ambitious Haman, whose power and influence are growing daily. Haman becomes further angered when Mordecai refuses to bow down to him as was the custom. In a classic villainous move, Haman tricks the king into ordering the massacre of all Jews in the empire in revenge for Mordecai's affront. This move put many in the empire in imminent danger— the date of the massacre had been broadcast throughout the land, and laws prohibited the overturning of a command that had been made in the name of the king.

While this plot developed, Esther sat in the king's palace. Mordecai had instructed her not to tell anyone that she was a Jew, so no one knew—not even the king. Mordecai realized that Esther was in a position to save her people, but she was reluctant to act. One could argue that Esther was afraid, and rightly so. Having been trained in the ways of the court, she was very aware of the risk to herself to even break the law forbidding her to approach the king, let alone intercede for a people sentenced to die. On the other hand, perhaps Esther simply could not imagine that her attempts to save her people could be effective. She had not yet realized that this was God's purpose for her.

The beauty of the following passage, Esther 4:4–17, is in Mordecai's clear challenge to Esther. Listen to the dialogue carried on through letters between these two—a wise old mentor and guardian, and a young woman whose life was in jeopardy.

> 4 When Esther's young women and her eunuchs came
> and told her, the queen was deeply distressed. She sent
> garments to clothe Mordecai, so that he might take off his
> sackcloth, but he would not accept them. 5 Then Esther

called for Hathach, one of the king's eunuchs, who had been appointed to attend her, and ordered him to go to Mordecai to learn what this was and why it was.

⁶ Hathach went out to Mordecai in the open square of the city in front of the king's gate, ⁷ and Mordecai told him all that had happened to him, and the exact sum of money that Haman had promised to pay into the king's treasuries for the destruction of the Jews. ⁸ Mordecai also gave him a copy of the written decree issued in Susa for their destruction, that he might show it to Esther and explain it to her and command her to go to the king to beg his favor and plead with him on behalf of her people.

⁹ And Hathach went and told Esther what Mordecai had said, ¹⁰ Then Esther spoke to Hathach and commanded him to go to Mordecai and say, ¹¹ "All the king's servants and the people of the king's provinces know that if any man or woman goes to the king inside the inner court without being called, there is but one law—to be put to death, except the one to whom the king holds out the golden scepter so that he may live. But as for me, I have not been called to come in to the king these thirty days."

¹² And they told Mordecai what Esther had said, ¹³ Then Mordecai told them to reply to Esther, "Do not think to yourself that in the king's palace you will escape any more than all the other Jews. ¹⁴ For if you keep silent at this time, relief and deliverance will rise for the Jews from another place, but you and your father's house will perish. And who knows whether you have not come to the kingdom for such a time as this?"

¹⁵ Then Esther told them to reply to Mordecai, Mordecai, ¹⁶ "Go, gather all the Jews to be found in Susa, and hold a fast on my behalf, and do not eat or drink

for three days, night or day. I and my young women will also fast as you do. Then I will go to the king, though it is against the law, and if I perish, I perish." [17] Mordecai then went away and did everything as Esther had ordered him.

Accepting Her Calling

Mordecai's challenge to Esther speaks of *destiny*: *"And who knows whether you have not come to the kingdom for such a time as this?"* Mordecai's struggle was helping Esther to see who she was and what her purpose was. Esther's struggle was in accepting the reality of the principle mentioned in our previous chapter: "Everyone to whom much was given, of him much will be required" (Luke 12: 48b). Esther's response signifies her victory through faith and her acceptance of her own role in history: "I will go to the king, though it is against the law, and if I perish, I perish!"

Working with God

Esther immediately put her decision into action. She went into three days of fasting and prayer along with all of her attendants and Jews throughout the nation. She then executed a plan. After gaining an audience with the king, she convinces him to hold a banquet where Haman would be a guest. Her intent is to expose the plot that had been designed to trick the king into invoking the death sentence upon the Jews.

But as Esther worked, God also was at work. Unable to sleep one night, the king reviews several royal reports and discovers that sometime earlier a man had warned the king of a plot to kill him. The king is astounded to learn that the man had not been rewarded for his act, and he asks Haman to suggest an appropriate way for the king to bestow honor on someone. Thinking that the king intends to honor *him*, Haman suggests a way that the man might bask in the accolades of the people. Imagine Haman's shock, humiliation, and fury when he had to honor Mordecai as he himself had hoped to be honored!

Meanwhile, plans for the banquet had proceeded. The king, still enthralled with Esther, asked her what she desired from him (for he had promised to grant her wish), and Esther told the king the entire plot to destroy her and her people.

The king's response was swift. Haman was immediately taken out and executed. Esther rose to the occasion, stepping into her position of power—a position that had been ordained by God. Esther had been chosen to be queen, and that turned out to be a position from which she could protect her people. However, that positioning had not been immediately apparent to her. It took circumstances, even crises, to prompt Esther to action.

When we must wrestle past our own fears and seize the opportunities we have been given, we come to realize the power God has given us through our position, His favor, and opportunity. When the situation is clarified, we are emboldened to accept God's calling and to claim the destiny we were designed to fill. Esther had to look beyond the obvious protocols, such as lack of access to the king, and do that which needed to be done. In the end, Haman was executed, Mordecai was elevated to a position of honor and responsibility, and a new decree was issued that allowed the Jews to defend themselves. God's people were preserved.

The beauty of this story lies in how God orchestrates circumstances on several levels while we continue to wrestle with who we are and what we are to do with His blessings. He uses the plots of others to support our development for greater use by Him. Frequently, our struggles are internal ones wherein we must face our own insecurities, then step out on the promises that God's Word has given us.

Reflection to Strengthen You for Your Struggle
What was Esther's struggle?
What did Esther's struggle teach her about the nature of God?
What was the impact of Esther's struggle on her?

What was the impact of Esther's struggle on others?

How does Esther's experience with God in her struggle relate to your life?

Hannah: Gaining by Letting Go

1 Samuel 1–2

If you've ever experienced or seen the pain of a woman who wants to know the joys of motherhood, and has not been able to become a mother, then you'll be able to grasp the depth of the hurt in a woman named Hannah. Her story is told in the first chapter of 1 Samuel. Hannah was married to a loving husband, who in keeping with the cultural traditions of the day, had two wives. His other wife had two children, but Hannah was barren. Scripture makes clear that it was God who had closed Hannah's womb; God was the source of her barrenness.

A Seemingly Endless Struggle

Once a year Hannah traveled with her husband to Shiloh, where the family obediently sacrificed to God. Her husband lovingly assured her that he still loved her and was committed to her happiness, despite her barren condition. During the offering, he even gave her a double portion of what she was due, again demonstrating his love for her.

Despite her husband's support, Hannah had to endure the daily taunting of her husband's other wife. Hannah was miserable as this pattern continued year after year. Most of us have experienced a moment or a circumstance in our lives that came to be unbearable simply because no end seemed to be in sight. We have told ourselves over and over again that doing without our heart's desire is all right; that we don't really need that thing or that circumstance; that we are strong, we can handle it. But the truth is that we are hurting and we want one specific solution. We can identify with this struggle.

Revealing Deep Hurt

Hannah's anguish drives her to a moment of utter despair as she finds herself crying out to God, pouring out her heart alone in the temple. But she soon discovers that she is not alone! Her experience is recorded in 1 Samuel 1:9–14, below:

> 9 After they had eaten and drunk in Shiloh, Hannah
> rose. Now Eli the priest was sitting on the seat beside the
> doorpost of the temple of the Lord. 10 She was deeply
> distressed and prayed to the Lord and wept bitterly. 11 And
> she vowed a vow and said, "O Lord of hosts, if you will
> indeed look on the affliction of your servant
> and remember me and not forget your servant, but will
> give to your servant a son, then I will give him to the
> Lord all the days of his life, and no razor shall touch his
> head."
>
> 12 As she continued praying before the Lord, Eli
> observed her mouth. 13 Hannah was speaking in her heart;
> only her lips moved, and her voice was not heard.
> Therefore Eli took her to be a drunken woman. 14 And
> Eli said to her, "How long will you go on being drunk? Put
> your wine away from you."

Desperation causes us to shed the trappings of emotional modesty that we often wrap around ourselves. Struggle causes us to drop our masquerade and show our real selves, to pour out our thoughts and feelings, and to confess who we really are and what we really need. While this can be uncomfortable, even frightening, it can be a true benefit of struggle. We spend so much time meeting societal expectations and our own personal expectations of ourselves, that we often become great pretenders, accomplished actors. Serious struggles push us out of our comfort zone and force us to say, "I am hurting, and *I need help!*"

The dialogue between Hannah and Eli, the priest, continues in 1 Samuel 1:15–18.

> [15] But Hannah answered, "No, my lord, I am a woman troubled in spirit. I have drunk neither wine nor strong drink, but I have been pouring out my soul before the LORD. [16] Do not regard your servant as a worthless woman, for all along I have been speaking out of my great anxiety and vexation." [17] Then Eli answered, "Go in peace, and the God of Israel grant your petition that you have made to him." [18] And she said, "Let your servant find favor in your eyes." Then the woman went her way and ate, and her face was no longer sad.

Peace and Other Blessings

The first result of Hannah's struggle, and of her sharing her true feelings with the priest and before God, is a sense of peace and assurance. For the first time in a long time, Hannah is at peace with her situation. As you read 1 Samuel 1:19–26, below, notice that Hannah feels a sense of peace even though her situation has not yet changed.

> [19] They [Hannah and her husband] rose early in the morning and worshiped before the LORD; then they went back to their house at Ramah. And Elkanah knew Hannah his wife, and the LORD remembered her. [20] And in due time Hannah conceived and bore a son, and she called his name Samuel, for she said, "I have asked for him from the LORD."
>
> [21] The man Elkanah and all his house went up to offer to the LORD the yearly sacrifice and to pay his vow. [22] But Hannah did not go up, for she said to her husband, "As soon as the child is weaned, I will bring him, so that he

may appear in the presence of the LORD and dwell there forever." 23 Elkanah her husband said to her, "Do what seems best to you; wait until you have weaned him; only, may the LORD establish His word." So the woman remained and nursed her son until she weaned him.

24 And when she had weaned him, she took him up with her, along with a three-year-old bull, an ephah of flour, and a skin of wine, and she brought him to the house of the LORD at Shiloh. And the child was young. 25 Then they slaughtered the bull, and they brought the child to Eli. 26 And she said, "Oh, my lord! As you live, my lord, I am the woman who was standing here in your presence, praying to the LORD. 27 For this child I prayed, and the LORD has granted me my petition that I made to Him. 28 Therefore I have lent him to the LORD. As long as he lives, he is lent to the LORD."

And he worshiped the LORD there.

Part of God's Perfect Plan

Hannah gave birth to a son and promptly honored her promise to give the child back to God as a servant. This was only the beginning of God's answer to Hannah. He blessed her with several children after Samuel. Samuel, however, remained committed to serving God in the temple as Eli's servant and protégé.

What ought we to learn from Hannah's experience? The passage points out that God was in control for the entire period of time—that Hannah's barrenness came from Him, and that her ability to have a child also came from Him. God is sovereign. And His timing is always perfect as He unfolds His plan for His people.

At that time in history, God's people needed an authentic prophet to speak to them and a man of integrity to walk before them. While God had used the prophet Eli in this role, Eli had failed to discipline his own sons, now destined to serve beside him, and later, as Eli became older, to serve in his place. Eli's sons were corrupt, and Eli was aware of their corrupt character, but he refused to confront them. The people had suffered under the sons' influence; the people needed a true prophet.

When the time was right according to God's plan, God sent a prophet, using Hannah to bring that prophet into the world. Hannah's struggle prepared her to totally submit to God's plan. Her conflict prepared her to be accepting of what was required in the future, even though she had no idea of what that future would hold. Divine circumstances were orchestrated to create a heart of obedience in Hannah so that she would indeed give this son of hers to be the prophet that God wanted for His people. As a result of the granting of her heart's desire for a child, Hannah was willing to give God's great gift back to Him. Hannah could praise God for having given her a son—yet she could willingly give up her son to God! Only God's working in her heart could prepare her to do such a thing.

Our struggles should teach us how to praise God for His manifest blessings. They should teach us how to pray fervently and learn to *yield to the will of God*. Our struggles must bring us to the point of seeing ourselves as part of a plan much larger than ourselves—a plan that is not about us, but about others—yet features a role for us to play as the plan unfolds.

Reflection to Strengthen You for Your Struggle
What was Hannah's struggle?
What did Hannah's struggle teach her about the nature of God?
What was the impact of Hannah's struggle on her?
What was the impact of Hannah's struggle on others?
How does Hannah's experience with God in his struggle relate to your life?

Gideon: Struggling to Live the "Life Unimagined"

Judges 6–8

Even as we struggle with our fear, God is moving in our life. This is perfectly illustrated in the life of Gideon, whose story is found in Judges 6–8. Gideon was from a small tribe of a defeated people. The children of Israel had fallen into a cycle of self-destructive behavior. Generation after generation had pledged obedience to God and had then conformed to the culture and practices of the nonbelievers around them.

A once-proud people who claimed a direct relationship with the true and living God of Scripture now found themselves living in caves, hiding out from a vicious enemy who annually attacked them and took everything that they had produced— from grain to cattle. The nation of Israel had resigned themselves to living a defeated life. They had settled for less, disregarding their heritage, their history, and their relationship with God. They had settled.

Living in Hopelessness

Maintaining our aspirations is indeed a struggle. The current reality, and even recent history, will declare to us that where we are is as good as it's going to get. "Get used to it! This is where you are, and this is all you'll ever be!" These are the messages that society and the culture frequently send us, and our believing these myths (no matter how daunting and real the current situation appears to be) can cause us to live out our lives in quiet desperation.

Much has been written about the levels of unhappiness and dissatisfaction that many in our society currently endure. Many people feel that they were meant for better, but they get up daily and continue doing that which they hate. They feel trapped, unfulfilled, without purpose, and ultimately without hope.

Living in Fear

The Bible introduces us to Gideon in Judges 6:11.

> Now the angel of the LORD came and sat under the terebinth at Ophrah, which belonged to Joash the Abiezrite, while his son Gideon was beating out wheat in the winepress to hide it from the Midianites.

Gideon's actions are typical of someone living a fearful life. He is hiding while performing his task, fearful that the enemy may come and take what is his. Rather than having servants do the work, he is doing it himself in order to maintain secrecy. Rather than using the power of oxen—the most efficient way to get the job done—he is doing the labor himself lest some animal make noise and draw attention to him. In every respect, Gideon is working so as to draw as little attention to himself as possible.

While living in fear, Gideon had settled into a mundane life of common tasks. How easily any of us can fall into this pattern! Gideon knows what the Israelites' enemy, the Midianites, are capable of. He understands the dangers of standing up, so safety was always a primary concern for him.

There was no problem with the work Gideon was doing—it simply wasn't the job for which he was destined. The winepress would not free his people from the oppression of the Midianites, would not allow him to grow as a man, would not allow him to communicate with God on a higher level, would not affect the lives of others in a profound way.

The angel comes and lingers under a tree; however, Gideon, engaged in his task, doesn't notice. God comes so unobtrusively to this man. The people of Israel had been praying for deliverance for about sixty-five years, and now God is preparing to act. The angel appears while Gideon is busy living his cautious life.

God comes to people in various ways—ways that will be meaningful to each of us so that we can grasp His message. Some of us need a quiet voice; some of us need to be knocked to the ground; some of us need a burning bush. Some of us get smoke and thunder, while others get the still small voice. Yet God *does* come! In Psalm 95:7–8 the psalmist says, "He is our God. . . Today, if you hear His voice, do not harden your hearts."The first question is "Do you listen?" The next question is "What is your response?"

Talking with God

In Judges 6:12 we see what happens next with Gideon and the angel: "And the angel of the LORD appeared to him and said to him, 'The LORD is with you, O mighty man of valor.'"

In this moment God speaks to Gideon through the angel, assuring Gideon that he is connected with the God of the universe. Knowing that God is by his side might have emboldened Gideon, but he needs even more. God then tells Gideon that he is a mighty man, a courageous man in God's sight. Mighty men are conquerors; they are brave, strong, and visionary. They are risk-takers. The angel conveys all of this in one ten-word sentence (in the quote above) while Gideon simply goes about his very mundane task, hiding out from an enemy that harasses his people.

We need to be sure that we understand the importance of what happened between Gideon and the angel—and realize that the same thing can happen to us. While we're waiting for something bigger to happen, God is speaking to us in that still small voice that is for us and us alone. God speaks destiny to us, no matter what our current state. He calls us sons and daughters. He calls us sanctified. He calls us a peculiar people, a royal priesthood. He calls us blessed. He declares that we are more than conquerors. He declares us righteous. God speaks to our potential, not to our present condition. God speaks to our purpose in life! God speaks to us within the struggle, whether that struggle is overt, such as David facing a giant; or internal, such as Gideon's fear.

When God spoke to Gideon, He first assured Gideon of His presence. Then He spoke to what that assurance would mean to Gideon. Too often we make the mistake of beginning with ourselves, rather than with God.

Gideon had a number of questions for God in Judges 6:13.

> And Gideon said to him, "Please, my lord, if the
> LORD is with us, why then has all this happened to us?
> And where are all His wonderful deeds that our fathers
> recounted to us, saying, 'Did not the LORD bring us up
> from Egypt?' But now the LORD has forsaken us and
> given us into the hand of Midian."

Gideon was basically asking, "If you are with us, why aren't we seeing miracles anymore? Why have our enemies defeated us?" Gideon had not dealt with his people's problem of sin, but God had. And God had now appeared in order to help His people's current situation with the Midianites.

In this direct conversation Gideon has the opportunity to question God. What he says, however, reveals that Gideon's present condition falls short of his potential. Although Gideon acknowledges what God has said, he is primarily *looking backward* and dwelling on the past. A healthier attitude for a visionary "mighty man of valor" would be to look toward the future, to have the attitude that Paul commends in Philippians 3:13b–14: "Forgetting those things which are behind and reaching forth unto those things which are before, I press towards the mark of the high calling of God in Christ Jesus." Such should be the position of a person being spoken to by God. Rather than wasting time, the person must seek to become future-oriented as quickly as possible in order to hasten realization of the future that God has planned and promised. Don't be stuck in your past!

God's Mission for Gideon

God reveals His mission for Gideon in Judges 6:14–17.

> 14 And the LORD turned to him and said, "Go in this might of yours and save Israel from the hand of Midian, do not I send you?" 15 And he said to Him, "Please, Lord, how can I save Israel? Behold, my clan is the weakest in Manasseh, and I am the least in my father's house." 16 And the LORD said to him, "But I will be with you, and you shall strike the Midianites as one man." 17 And he said to Him, "If now I have found favor in your eyes, then show me a sign that it is you who speaks with me.

God doesn't address Gideon's run of excuses and questions. It's as if He knows that Gideon is so locked into his narrow thinking that he can't even hear what's being said. "Go [marching orders] in this might [the power of the almighty God within you] because you are going to defeat an enemy for your people." God provides not only a clear command and assurance of His presence, but also a guarantee of the battle's outcome.

Responding to God's Commands

When we have been stuck in small thinking for a long time, or ensnared in a particular circumstance, it can be difficult for us to immediately step into what God has already ordained for us. People's various responses can be attributed to their personal makeup and their past experiences.

The story of Gideon continuously challenges me. I wonder what has been the cost of narrow thinking in my own life. When have I been slow to hear what God has said to me? It isn't that I've missed anything that I needed to do. The timetable is God's. In each situation, God's plan went forward just as He had ordained it. My concern is that I recognize that I am in the same struggling mode, with God still speaking to me about my own call to serve.

Let me be even more personal for a moment. I believe that God challenged me earlier in my life. He said to me, "I promise you long life, challenge, and victory in *me*." Given those promises and the gifts that God has given me, what are the challenges that I ought to be seeing and be confronting during my life? What limits am I placing on myself? Am I busy doing winepress work while God is calling me to something larger? Has He not already told me that mine would be a "life unimagined"? Has He not said to me, "I will come when you call. I am God, and I fail not. I will give you the desires of your heart, and I have heard your heart's cry."

Yes, God has said all of these things to me—and to you. It's time for us to re-envision the world before us. God has given us the blessing of life, the chance to do that which we have been putting off for years.

In 2 Timothy 1:6–7, Paul wrote, "For this reason I remind you to fan into flame the gift of God, which is in you through the laying on of my hands, for God gave us a spirit not of fear but of power and love and self-control." Paul is admonishing Timothy to recognize his God-given gifts, which he ought to be using. In a sense, to fail to use such gifts is direct disobedience to God. Paul goes on to remind Timothy that if a spirit of timidity is hampering the use of his gifts, that spirit is not from God. A clear distinction is drawn here between timidity and humility. To have fear and reverence for God is humility. To fail to go forward and do what God has ordained, even *commanded* for you to do, is an act of disobedience.

Finally Gideon begins to see beyond the winepress of his current existence and accept the possibility of God's call on his life. He is right to acknowledge his humble background, but he has yet to grasp that a humble background is merely the womb within which many of us have developed. God immediately dispels Gideon's misgivings with His reassurance of His presence and with even more detail about Gideon's mission: "I will be with you, and you shall strike the Midianites as one man." That is the power of the assurance of the presence of God; there is no ambiguity in God's description of the outcome!

Gideon moved from his internal struggle with fear and an inability to see himself as God saw him, to beginning to face the mission that God had placed before him. He wanted more proof, however, that the angel of the LORD was who He said He was. After the angel performed a miracle, Gideon was concerned because he realized that he had seen the LORD face to face. The LORD reassured him, however, saying, "Peace be to you. Do not fear; you shall not die" (Judges 6:23). God directly addressed Gideon's fear, the main issue that kept him from fulfilling God's plan for his life. In place of fear, God granted Gideon peace.

Despite various assurances from God, Gideon's struggle to act boldly was only just beginning. His first act of leadership was to tear down the altar of Baal, one of the false gods that was worshiped by local people, even by some Israelites. This act quickly aroused passion in the community and a demand for the offender to be killed. Word quickly got out that Gideon was the person who had torn down the altar. His first bold action had brought into question the power of Baal to fight for himself and to administer justice. When no response from Baal could be seen, word of Gideon's first exploit as a leader spread quickly among the Israelites.

Taking the first steps toward overcoming our fears is a crucial start toward becoming the person God has called us to be. Not only are our first small steps important to *us*, they also provide a vital example for those who will later follow us, giving them an opportunity to see what courage can look like in someone they know personally. This first step by Gideon caused him to be given a new name—a name indicative of the warrior that God had ordained him to be, the person that others would follow into battle.

Preparing for Battle

Gideon asked for even *more* assurance that God would give the Israelites victory over the Midianites. First he asked that a fleece laid on the ground would be wet with dew while the ground remained dry. God met that request. Gideon then asked for the reverse—that there would be dew on the ground while the fleece remained dry. Again God fulfilled Gideon's request.

As Gideon began to live out his destiny, the text is clear that he still had his fears. However, the powerful aspect of this story is that God sees us as finished even while we are still developing, and He empowers us to act based upon who we are becoming. God leads Gideon to go and spy on the enemy forces, and from his vantage point, he hears the enemy talking about a dream that one of them had just experienced. In the dream, a loaf of bread rolls into the Midianites' camp and flattens a tent. Both Gideon and the Midianites interpret the dream in the same way—as a sign of the Midianites' defeat and Gideon's victory.

Gideon returns from his reconnaissance mission with the assurance that God has given him victory in the minds of his enemy. All he needs to do is to go forth and claim the victory. If Gideon acts in obedience, God will deliver the enemy into his hands as if they are one man!

The struggle, however, continues. Originally Gideon had 32,000 men in his command. However, God directs Gideon to reduce his troops to 10,000 and then to 300—an absurdly low number to fight a battle. Then God gives Gideon the most extraordinary tactical plan for facing the enemy: to carry horns, pitchers, and lights to face a mortal enemy.

Even for a new military leader, this surely felt insane. But, along the way, Gideon had come to consult God and had seen God speak to him in amazing ways, assuring him of victories that could occur only supernaturally. If this were to be a victory, it would *have* to be supernatural!

As we face insurmountable odds, as we look with our natural eye rather than with our spiritual eye, as we may see resources disappear just when they seem to be most important to us—our personal struggle is to face our battles trusting that God will do the supernatural. For when God does the supernatural, we know for certain with whom true power lies. Our struggle is to accept the fact that the battle is not ours—it is the Lord's!

Reflection to Strengthen You for Your Struggle

What was Gideon's struggle?

What did Gideon's struggle teach him about the nature of God?

What was the impact of Gideon's struggle on him?

What was the impact of Gideon's struggle on others?

How does Gideon's experience with God in his struggle relate to your life?

Elijah: Standing Alone for Principle

1 Kings 17–19

Of the many stories in Scripture that teach us about standing alone for principle, none contains more boldness than the story of Elijah facing off against the prophets of Baal. As a prophet, Elijah often had to stand against rampant idolatry among his own people—an idolatry fueled by the passions of kings who had long ago ceased to honor God.

Standing Alone for God

At one point Elijah felt certain that he was the last person standing for God. Then God revealed to him that there were, in fact, many who had not bowed to the pressure of society and the king. To capture the attention of the people, God instructed Elijah to tell the king that there would be a drought—no rain for several years. This crippled the nation, but it demonstrated the power of the true God. After about three years, a confrontation took place between Elijah and the prophets of Baal—450 of them facing one man with faith, and the power of God within him.

The confrontation began with Elijah issuing a challenge to the people. In essence, he presented them with a choice: "If the LORD is God, follow Him; but if Baal, then follow him" (1 Kings 18:21b). Elijah was pushing the people to make a choice.

The people did not respond to this challenge, so Elijah set up a confrontation to settle once and for all the question of who had ultimate power, the God of Israel or the pagan Baal. Elijah boldly declared that while he was the only prophet of Israel's God in attendance, Baal had 450 prophets in attendance. The face-off involving the sacrifice of two bulls as offerings is recounted in 1 Kings 18:21–40. The God who demonstrated power would be recognized as the true God.

[22] Then Elijah said to the people, ". . . [23] Let two bulls be given to us, and let them choose one bull for themselves and cut it in pieces and lay it on the wood, but put no fire to it. And I will prepare the other bull and lay it on the wood and put no fire to it. [24] And you call upon the name of your god, and I will call upon the name of the LORD, and the God who answers by fire, He is God." And all the people answered, "It is well spoken." [25] Then Elijah said to the prophets of Baal, "Choose for yourselves one bull and prepare it first, for you are many, and call upon the name of your god, but put no fire to it."

[26] And they took the bull that was given them, and they prepared it and called upon the name of Baal from morning until noon, saying, "O Baal, answer us!" But there was no voice, and no one answered. And they limped around the altar that they had made. [27] And at noon Elijah mocked them, saying, "Cry aloud, for he is a god. Either he is musing, or he is relieving himself, or he is on a journey, or perhaps he is asleep and must be awakened."

[28] And they cried aloud and cut themselves after their custom with swords and lances, until the blood gushed out upon them. [29] And as midday passed, they raved on until the time of the offering of the oblation, but there was no voice. No one answered; no one paid attention.

[30] Then Elijah said to all the people, "Come near to me." And all the people came near to him. And he repaired the altar of the LORD that had been thrown down. [31] Elijah took twelve stones, according to the

number of the tribes of the sons of Jacob, to whom the word of the LORD came, saying, "Israel shall be your name," [32] and with the stones he built an altar in the name of the LORD. And he made a trench about the altar, as great as would contain two seahs of seed. [33] And he put the wood in order and cut the bull in pieces and laid it on the wood. And he said, "Fill four jars with water and pour it on the burnt offering and on the wood." [34] And he said, "Do it a second time." And they did it a second time. And he said, "Do it a third time." And they did it a third time. [35] And the water ran around the altar and filled the trench also with water.

[36] And at the time of the offering of the oblation, Elijah the prophet came near and said, "O LORD, God of Abraham, Isaac, and Israel, let it be known this day that you are God in Israel, and that I am your servant, and that I have done all these things at your word. [37] Answer me, O LORD, answer me, that this people may know that you, O LORD, are God, and that you have turned their hearts back." [38] Then the fire of the LORD fell and consumed the burnt offering and the wood and the stones and the dust, and licked up the water that was in the trench. [39] And when all the people saw it, they fell on their faces and said, "The LORD, He is God; the LORD, He is God." [40] And Elijah said to them, "Seize the prophets of Baal; let not one of them escape." And they seized them. And Elijah brought them down to the brook Kishon and slaughtered them there.

The daunting task of standing alone against many is a true test of who we are and of the principles we live by. Standing before a nation of people and directing them to make a decision about who they are and (in the case of the Israelites) *whose* they are—who they worship and who they trust—was not a challenge to be issued by the faint of heart. However, in nearly every struggle at some point it becomes necessary to stand alone.

Elijah's history with God, his communion with God, and his personal experiences with God (at his times of weakness as well as at his times of strength) prepared him for his challenge with the prophets of Baal. This struggle pushed Elijah to act with conviction. It caused him to boldly and thoroughly trust that God would powerfully present Himself. And Elijah himself was immersed in the purpose of God as he laid the challenge first before the Israelites and then before those who worshiped the false prophets.

Benefits of Standing Alone

Standing alone refines and strengthens the quality of our integrity. Standing on what others cannot see increases our faith in the God we have chosen. Standing alone clarifies what we say we believe and what we are willing to risk in order to lead others to share our beliefs. The struggle of standing alone can indeed change the course of a people and a nation.

Standing on Principle in Recent Times

An excellent illustration of this idea of standing for principle occurred in the life of a contemporary cultural leader, the Reverend Dr. Martin Luther King, Jr. During the latter years of the civil rights movement in the United States, the war in Vietnam was at its highest point. As Dr. King looked at this war, he became more and more convinced of the fact that this was an unjust war. His conviction wouldn't necessarily have become an issue, but because of his conviction, he felt compelled to speak out against the war.

Starting in 1965 Dr. King began to argue his case in national media, on talk shows, and in speeches. Dr. King felt that the war took money and resources that could have been allocated to fighting the war on poverty and to alleviating other social concerns in America. The United States was spending more and more money on the military and less and less on the anti-poverty programs of the day. On April 4, 1967, exactly one year before his death, Dr. King delivered a speech titled "Beyond Vietnam: A Time to Break Silence." Following are some excerpts from that speech:[1]

A true revolution of values will soon look uneasily on the glaring contrast of poverty and wealth. With righteous indignation, it will look across the seas and see individual capitalists of the West investing huge sums of money in Asia, Africa and South America, only to take the profits out with no concern for the social betterment of the countries, and say: "This is not just."

A nation that continues year after year to spend more money on military defense than on programs of social uplift is approaching spiritual death.

True compassion is more than flinging a coin to a beggar. It comes to see that an edifice which produces beggars needs restructuring.

We were taking the young black men who had been crippled by our society and sending them eight thousand miles away to guarantee liberties which they had not found in southwest Georgia and East Harlem. So we have been repeatedly faced with the cruel irony of watching Negro and white boys on TV screens as they kill and die together for a nation that has been unable to seat them together in the same schools.

Dr. King's position against the Vietnam War cost him a number of allies. His own lieutenants in the civil rights movement admonished him to be quiet; otherwise he would risk destroying relationships with their few remaining allies. President Johnson, union leaders, and publishers declared that Dr. King had diminished his value to the civil rights movement, to his country, and to his cause.

My objective is not to defend the validity of Dr. King's position, but rather to use his stance to point out that there are still moments in contemporary times that require us to take a stand against the masses, against the conventional wisdom. There are times when we must be willing to say provocative things that might move people to make moral choices.

On what issues are you being challenged to take a stand? How will you respond to this opportunity? What are you prepared to risk in order to stand for what you know is the right thing to say or do? Is your position on this issue consistent with God's Word? Could you stand for this issue if God were the only one supporting you?

Reflection to Strengthen You for Your Struggle
What was Elijah's struggle?
What did Elijah's struggle teach him about the nature of God?
What was the impact of Elijah's struggle on him?
What was the impact of Elijah's struggle on others?
How does Elijah's experience with God in his struggle relate to your life?

1. https://kinginstitute.stanford.edu/king-papers/documents/beyond-vietnam

Moses: Strength Made Perfect in Weakness

Exodus 2–6

The story of Moses and his encounter with God in the wilderness is well known and unique. Following a decree that all male Hebrew infants in the land were to be killed, Moses' mother placed him on the Nile River in a makeshift boat, hoping that God would somehow preserve his life.

As providence would have it, Pharaoh's daughter rescued Moses from the river, immediately loved him, and sought her father's permission to keep him. Moses' own mother was actually hired to care for Moses during his upbringing. Moses was raised as an Egyptian and nurtured as a Hebrew. Moses was truly a man of two worlds—Egyptian on the outside and Hebrew on the inside.

Champion of Justice for the Hebrews in Egypt

Even as a child, Moses had a strong sense of justice and experienced a desire to liberate the Hebrew people from Egyptian bondage. It seemed inevitable that he would someday be moved to action. As a young man, Moses one day found himself witnessing an Egyptian physically abusing a Hebrew. He quickly stepped into the conflict and killed the oppressor; then he buried the body. His problem suddenly became worse when, the very next day, he found himself intervening in a dispute between two Hebrews. As he challenged the man in the wrong, that man responded with an underlying accusation: "Who made you a prince and a judge over us? Do you mean to kill me as you killed the Egyptian?" (Exodus 2:14).

Preparation Among the Hebrews

Moses fled, recognizing that the killing he had considered secret was not secret at all. Realizing that it was only a matter of time until he would be held accountable for his crime, Moses fled to Midian, where he lived among Hebrews. He stayed there for forty years, marrying a Hebrew woman and tending sheep. This season in Moses' life provided a long time for him to meditate and for God to prepare him for the work to come—liberating his people from the Egyptians.

Moses seemed to have inherent courage to face an enemy and to fight for the oppressed, even when those actions involved putting himself at risk. What Moses lacked was the patience and wisdom needed to lead and liberate his people most effectively. Moses' zeal and righteous indignation against injustice, his struggle with the Egyptian, and his confrontation with his own Hebrew brothers propelled him into a season of preparation for what would become his life's calling: freeing his people—God's people. Often, our first struggles merely set the stage for us to begin the training for our major calling.

Encountering God Face to Face

In the fortieth year following his flight from Egypt, Moses had a personal encounter with God. This intense experience became the beginning of his greatest struggle: the leading of his people out of Egyptian bondage. One day Moses observed an extraordinary phenomenon: a bush burning without being consumed. As Moses drew closer, he heard the command from God: "Do not come near; take your sandals off your feet, for the place on which you are standing is holy ground" (Exodus 3:5).

Moses recognized the presence of God. However, he was shocked when God directed him to go and free his people. Moses had long wanted his people to be free; however, he hadn't considered that *he* would play a role in their liberation. Now God was *commanding* him to *lead* them! In Exodus 4:10–16 we see Moses' own doubt and self-image preventing him from immediately accepting God's command.

> 10 But Moses said to the LORD, "Oh, my Lord, I am
> not eloquent, either in the past or since you have spoken
> to your servant, but I am slow of speech and of tongue."
> 11 Then the LORD said to him, "Who has made man's
> mouth? Who makes him mute, or deaf, or seeing, or blind?
> Is it not I, the LORD? 12 Now therefore go, and I will be
> with your mouth and teach you what you shall speak."
> 13 But he said, "Oh, my Lord, please send someone else."
> 14 Then the anger of the LORD was kindled against Moses
> and He said, "Is there not Aaron, your brother, the Levite?
> I know that he can speak well. Behold, he is coming out to
> meet you, and when he sees you, he will be glad in his
> heart. 15 You shall speak to him and put the words in his
> mouth, and I will be with your mouth and with his mouth
> and will teach you both what to do. 16 He shall speak for
> you to the people, and he shall be your mouth, and you
> shall be as God to him.

God proceeded to demonstrate His power to Moses through two miracles—first turning Moses' rod into a snake, then back to a rod; and next turning Moses' hand leprous and then healthy again. Even with those manifestations—and help from God Himself and from Aaron, Moses still doubted his suitability for this task.

This is truly one of the great internal struggles: having the confidence to allow our actions to rise to the level of what God calls us to be. How many times have we failed to accept opportunities before us because of our own doubt or lack of confidence? God often calls us to massive tasks that are indeed outside our meager human grasp, but the presence, power, and preservation of God assure us of victory. It is appropriate for us to acknowledge our shortcomings, but we must believe that God will not allow those shortcomings to prevent us from accomplishing God's will. In fact, our inadequacies can even be an advantage: In 2 Corinthians 12:9, Paul writes that Jesus told him, "My power is made perfect in weakness." When we are willing to surrender our weakness and let the power of Christ work through us, amazing things can be accomplished.

Sometimes our struggle simply involves our recognizing that two seemingly contradictory ideas can simultaneously be true: On one hand, we are not able, in and of ourselves, to accomplish the great tasks that God may place before us; yet on the other hand, we must stand on God's promise that Paul states in Philippians 4:13—"I can do all things through Him [Christ] who strengthens me." Reconciling these two truths can indeed be a struggle.

As Moses was making his excuses, God was moving—putting Moses' brother Aaron in place to be the spokesman for the mission. Moses' fundamental struggle, even prior to his audience with Pharaoh, was to fully grasp the reality that all things are possible with God—to realize that God equips those He calls.

Advocating in the Strength of God

Exodus records that Moses went before Pharaoh ten times with God's command to let the Hebrews go. After the first appeal, Pharaoh retaliated by making the Hebrews' labor more arduous. He cut their supply of straw needed to make bricks, at the same time maintaining the quota of bricks the people were required to make. When the people asked their masters about this change, blame was placed on Moses. Moses' demand had led to his people suffering even more!

As we can see in Exodus 5:21–6:9, below, Moses struggled with this result. First the foremen in charge of the Israelites were angry with him. Then Moses complained to God:

21 And they [the foremen] said to them [Moses and Aaron], "The Lord look on you and judge, because you have made us stink in the sight of Pharaoh and his servants, and have put a sword in their hand to kill us." 22 Then Moses turned to the Lord and said, "O Lord, why have you done evil to this people? Why did you ever send me? 23 For since I came to Pharaoh to speak in your name, he has done evil to this people, and you have not delivered your people at all."

1But the Lord said to Moses, "Now you shall see what I will do to Pharaoh; for with a strong hand he will send them out, and with a strong hand he will drive them out of his land."

2 God spoke to Moses and said to him, "I am the Lord. 3 I appeared to Abraham, to Isaac, and to Jacob, as God Almighty, but by my name the Lord I did not make myself known to them. 4 I also established my covenant with them to give them the land of Canaan, the land in which they lived as sojourners. sojourners. 5 Moreover, I have heard the groaning of the people of Israel whom the Egyptians hold as slaves, and I have remembered my covenant. 6 Say therefore to the people of Israel, 'I am the Lord, and I will bring you out from under the burdens of the Egyptians, and I will deliver you from slavery to them, and I will redeem you with an outstretched arm and with great acts of judgment. 7 I will take you to be my people, and I will be your God, and you shall know that I am the Lord your God, who has brought you out from under the burdens of the Egyptians. 8 I will bring you into the land that I swore to give to Abraham, to Isaac, and to Jacob. I will give it to you for a possession. I am the Lord.'" 9 Moses spoke thus to the people of Israel,

but they did not listen to Moses, because of their broken spirit and harsh slavery.

Moses warned Pharaoh about nine plagues that God would inflict on Egypt. These plagues cut at the religious and economic core of the Egyptians. Nevertheless, Pharaoh continued to oppress the Hebrew people. Finally, the tenth plague—the death of the firstborn of all creatures in the nation, including humans—broke the will of Pharaoh, who freed the Hebrews, sending them away with riches. Pharaoh soon changed his mind and sent his army in pursuit of the Hebrews. This caused many Egyptian soldiers to be drowned in the Red Sea, which had parted for the Hebrews.

Moses' Specific Challenges

In order for Moses to fulfill God's mission—to free the Hebrew people from their slavery in Egypt—he had needed to endure the struggle of tempering his impetuous nature with patience and wisdom. God provided him with many specific challenges along the way:

- To accept a role that was far beyond his own capabilities
- To acknowledge his weaknesses and then obey, trusting that God would provide what he needed
- To stand before a powerful enemy who had disdain for him, his God, and his people
- To watch through the plagues, seeing Pharaoh disregard God's commandments and heap further hardships on the Hebrew people
- To face the scorn and frustration of his own people as they paid the price for his bold obedience to God

Important Lessons That Moses Learned

Like his people—and all of *us*—Moses needed to learn the following during his struggle:

- God is in full control.

- God knows us completely and has already planned how to deal with our weaknesses.
- Our God is a personal, covenant-keeping God.
- God has the power and the will to deliver what He promises.

Reflection to Strengthen You for Your Struggle
What was Moses' struggle?
What did Moses' struggle teach him about the nature of God?
What was the impact of Moses' struggle on him?
What was the impact of Moses' struggle on others?
How does Moses' experience with God in this struggle relate to your life?

Job: Accepting the Good and the Evil

Job 1–2

In Chapter 1 of the Book of Job, Job is presented to us as a model of the righteous man. Job was respected, affluent, a good husband and father. In addition, Job was devout, acting as the high priest of his household, praying and making sacrifices for his children as the ultimate intercessor.

Satan's Testing

Satan believed that Job was righteous and trusted in God only because he was wealthy and everything was going well for him. Satan wanted to test Job to see whether he would maintain his faith in God even in unfavorable circumstances. Such a test required God's permission, so Satan asked God to permit him to attack Job on various levels. God granted that permission; the only restriction God placed on Satan was that he was not to take Job's life.

In rapid succession, Job lost his property; he lost his servants; he lost his children; and then his body was attacked with disease. Job lost *much* in a very short period of time. He found himself mourning his losses and suffering from painful sores on his body. Job's wife saw her husband's anguish and, in Job 2:9–10, urged an extreme response:

> ⁹ Then his wife said to him, "Do you still hold fast your integrity? Curse God and die." ¹⁰ But he said to her, "You speak as one of the foolish women would

speak. Shall we receive good from God, and shall we not receive evil?" In all this Job did not sin with his lips.

What a crucial moment for Job! His wife, who loves him and suffers with him, cannot bear to see this good man suffer any longer. She had seen him faithfully lead and guide his family, seen him serve as the high priest of his household, seen him pray for her and others. Yet now she has witnessed the God Job worships allow everything to be taken from him and from her. She has her own pain—the loss of their children and their possessions—to deal with. And she has to watch the man she loves suffer tremendously.

Yet even in this moment, Job still worships God! His wife describes this moment as being about Job's integrity—and Job maintains that integrity, still acting as the high priest of the household, still holding on to who he is. As Job upholds his high standard of integrity, he challenges his wife to maintain that standard as well.

Job is about to learn something about himself, but he is about to learn even more about God! And Job's withstanding Satan's test enables each of us who reads his story to benefit from his experience. Job's story challenges each of us to examine where we stand in a moment of personal crisis. When the tsunami, the earthquake, the super tornado, the flood, the raging fire, the cancer, the AIDS strikes us, where will we stand in the moment of that struggle? When we see everything lost, and there is yet another wave, where will we stand?

Faith in the Struggle

Job teaches a fundamental lesson about our own attitude and the application of our faith in a time of struggle. We must remember our eagerness to accept good from God. That is human nature. However, storms do arise; struggles will surface. While this text clearly teaches that the storms do not originate with God, those storms *do* occur with His permission. And they arise with a purpose.

Job courageously states through his pain that we who accept the good things from God must also embrace the difficulties that He permits. This becomes easier if we remember the truth of Romans 8:28—"For those who love God all things work together for good, for those who are called according to His purpose." Truly Job's question is the question of the moment and of the age: *"Shall we receive good from God, and shall we not receive evil?"* What a guideline!

Deeper Insight from Experience

A person can come to grasp spiritual insight through revelation or through intense study of Scripture. However, *experience* has a way of indelibly imprinting essential and difficult truths upon us. On the first level of an experience such as Job's, our struggle would involve dealing with the physical pain of affliction; the emotional and mental pain of losing loved ones, property, or even intangibles. At some point, however, we'd probably also need to confront the spiritual pain of attempting to understand a sovereign, loving God who would permit His beloved to experience such deep pain.

Job models this reality. He moves from standing faithfully in spite of the plea from his wife, to demanding an audience with God in order to present his case that he is being treated unjustly. It is only when God confronts Job that Job suddenly remembers who God is—and who he is. That realization causes Job to hurriedly step back. This struggle brings him to a new awareness of the sovereignty and power of God.

Consider the power of such awareness! Notice how Job's perspective on the wonder and power of God has been deepened by his own experience: "I had heard of you by the hearing of the ear, / but now my eye sees you" (Job 42:5). If we're to have an ever-deepening relationship with God, we need to understand who He is; we need to try to begin to fathom His power and His goodness and His love for us. We need to revere Him, to understand that His ways are different from our ways, and to worship Him for who He is. Job's struggle during this trial led him to a deeper understanding of God, and to repentance and restoration.

In some ways Job's experience is similar to Hagar's experience recorded in Genesis. It's one thing to *hear* about God, but to "see Him," to more deeply understand Him and the depths of both His love and His power, is more valuable than anything else we can possess. One of our greatest sources of peace of mind is the realization that God knows us completely, and He orchestrates experiences in our lives so that we can know *Him* more deeply. Additional peace of mind comes from knowing that God has the power to restore if that is His will. The Book of Job ends with God restoring to Job even more than had been taken from him, including children.

The more we understand about who God is, the more easily we can accept both the good and the bad that come to us in life. We might even find ourselves quoting a familiar declaration from Job: "The LORD gave, and the LORD has taken away; blessed be the name of the LORD" (Job 1:21b).

Reflection to Strengthen You for Your Struggle
What was Job's struggle?
What did Job's struggle teach him about the nature of God?
What was the impact of Job's struggle on him?
What was the impact of Job's struggle on others?
How does Job's experience with God in his struggle relate to your life?

Peter: Struggling to Maintain Focus

Matthew 14:22–33

I frequently feel myself challenged by the realization that I exhibit the failings of so many people written about in Scripture. And none convict me more than Peter.

A Storm as a Catalyst for Increased Faith

Peter's walking on water is a straightforward example of God using struggle to lead us to new levels of faith. The Apostles had just finished seeing Jesus pull fish from fish and bread from bread in order to feed the five thousand people who had come to hear Jesus preach. Luke records that even though the Apostles had witnessed this miracle, their hearts were hardened and they did not grasp the significance of the event. While they spoke of Jesus being the Messiah, they were still struggling to realize what that actually meant. And who can honestly blame them? God had never become man before. The Apostles were human beings with limited perspectives, and though they were saved and were becoming primary sources and eye witnesses of the fulfilling of Scripture, they had a learning curve.

Following the feeding of the five thousand and the collection of the leftovers from the meal, Jesus sends the multitudes away. He then sends the Apostles away as well, instructing them to cross to the other side of the Sea of Galilee while He goes into the mountains to pray. Shortly after they cast off, a huge storm arises. While following the orders of Jesus, the Apostles find themselves in the midst of a huge storm. Such a point cannot be overlooked: That they found themselves in a huge storm *while* following the instructions of Jesus further illustrates how God uses the adversities of life to provide the best opportunities for instruction. He immerses us in active learning and then in one moment of time clarifies both His power and our need for Him. Believers often find themselves in the midst of a struggle as a result of their obedience to God. Daniel, whom we read about earlier in this book, is an example of that. It is one thing to be in a struggle as a result of disobedience, but another altogether to be in a struggle while being obedient to the will of God.

A storm on the Sea of Galilee was not a new phenomenon. Although the Apostles were experienced sailors, the intensity of this storm put them in peril. Imagine their surprise when, in the midst of their struggle, they saw Jesus walking on the water. At first they perceived Him to be some kind of phantom and cried out in fear. Matthew 14:27–29a tells us what happened next:

> 27 Immediately Jesus spoke to them, saying, "Take heart; it is I. Do not be afraid."
>
> 28 And Peter answered him, "Lord, if it is you, command me to come to you on the water."
>
> 29 He said, "Come."

Recognizing God in the Struggle

Storms and struggles often cause us to clarify whether it is God who is engaging us. Each of us has had a moment in our faith walk, when we have asked God, "Are you here? Are you near? Why can't I clearly see you in the midst of this turmoil?" Struggles often cause us to seek clarity about who we are and whom we believe in. Struggles cause us to become refocused on who God is, on His power, and on our need to get closer to Him.

I love the fact that this passage teaches us that God is in the storm *with* us, willing to hear us and able to empower us while we're in the storm *together.* Peter steps out of the boat and begins an improbable, and seemingly impossible, journey toward Jesus. He is focused on who Jesus is and on what he is able to do when he is empowered by Christ. This is a theme that Paul often included in his later writing. In Philippians 4:19 he wrote, "I can do all things through Him [Christ] who strengthens me." And how well this demonstrates a quotation of Jesus from Luke 18:27—"What is impossible with men is possible with God."

Peter finds himself doing the impossible with power and assurance. He had stepped out of the boat into the supernatural. No matter how fragile the boat might have been, it still offered some comfort and protection from the storm. It was definitely more stable than walking on a stormy sea! But to leave the boat would seem to mean sure death from a very real storm—unless your eye was on the God who had made the storm.

Peter was walking with power—until the distractions came. At first Peter had focused upon Jesus, not on the surrounding conditions, but slowly the spray of the water, the tumult around him, the roar of the wind began to distract him, and as he became distracted, he began to sink! He cried out to Jesus, "Lord, save me!" and Jesus extended a hand to him, raising him up from the engulfing waves and walking him back to the boat where the other Apostles watched in amazement!

Deepened Understanding of God in the Struggle

The Apostles' realization of who was in their midst was beginning to crystallize. What the feeding of the five thousand had not done, this experience in the midst of the storm *did*: It heightened their awareness of Jesus as the Messiah, the Son of God—one who had the power to defy the laws of gravity and nature! Their Master was indeed God!

Jesus had always been the Messiah, God in the flesh, but Peter's *perception* of who He was, and of the power He possessed, was changed after this struggle. The natural challenge of fighting to

86

keep a boat afloat yielded to a powerful spiritual struggle for Peter. He might have thought, "If God can do *this*, He can do anything!" He might have wondered whether *he* could use the power of God to do supernatural things, whether it would be appropriate for him to ask the Lord to empower *him* to do the impossible.

Such a struggle of faith happens to us during moments of crisis. The struggle calls us to get out of our safety zone (our boat) and try the impossible (to walk on water). And the greater struggle occurs after we have actually begun to do the impossible (for example, to walk on water).

Struggle helps us understand the supernatural occurrences in our lives—the healing that occurs after a long illness; the job one gets after searching incessantly; the mercy that is shown by a perceived enemy; the second chance that is offered after one has made a devastating error. Struggle reminds us that there are forces that we have no control over—and that we have a Savior who hears our prayers.

When I first read Matthew 14, I became acutely aware that God hears our prayers in the storms of life; that He wants us to recognize Him in the midst of our turmoil; that He wants us to become closer to Him in our storms and struggles. God wants us to know that He will actually come to us in the midst of our struggles. He wants us to know that life has limitless possibilities if we seek a closer walk with Him. This is an amazing thought! He wants our struggles to lead us to moments of clarity about who He is and the praise He deserves for being God—and God alone.

During this experience, Peter learned what was personally possible through Jesus, and the Apostles came to understand that this Jesus was indeed powerful. God empowers, but our personal responsibility is to stay focused on the task before us. What truly excites me about this narrative is the reality that my feeble attempts to stay focused often fail, and when they do, I can still call on the

God who empowers me, and He will restore me *while the struggle is going on*!

Challenges as Stepping Stones

Ultimately challenges return in different forms. Based on what you now know about God (not about yourself), when the challenge returns, will you be wiser, stronger, more faithful, more daring, and bolder in your stands and your decisions?

Peter's stepping out of the boat turned out to be a rehearsal for the day he would stand and preach the gospel to thousands—and see three thousand give their lives to Christ. One event was as supernatural as the other. Walking on water was miraculous. A man who had once denied knowing Jesus now proclaiming Him to thousands, and seeing the thousands respond was just as miraculous. One man's life was saved when Jesus lifted Peter as he sank in the stormy sea, but thousands were saved when that one man proclaimed the message of salvation for the lost!

Our struggles become stepping stones—dry runs for the challenges to come. Surely this reality can help us to see God as we live out our lives and face our daily challenges.

Reflection to Strengthen You for Your Struggle
What was Peter's struggle?
What did Peter's struggle teach him about the nature of God?
What was the impact of Peter's struggle on him?
What was the impact of Peter's struggle on others?
How does Peter's experience with God in his struggle relate to your life?

When Struggle Seems Endless

Mark 5:22–34

Sometimes our struggle feels endless. A challenge becomes part of our everyday life, part of our very being. We exhaust resources, lose friends, and lose hope in the process of facing our daily challenge.

A Long Multifaceted Struggle

This woman with whom Jesus had a brief encounter had been dealing with a multifaceted challenge for a long time. Scripture provides few details about her, other than to say that she'd had an "issue of blood" for twelve years. Unpacking this short narrative (Mark 5:22–34) paints a vivid picture of the woman's plight.

> 25 And there was a woman who had had a discharge of blood for twelve years, 26 and who had suffered much under many physicians, and had spent all that she had, and was no better but rather grew worse. 27 She had heard the reports about Jesus and came up behind Him in the crowd and touched His garment. 28 For she said, "If I touch even His garments, I will be made well." 29 And immediately the flow of blood dried up, and she felt in her body that she was healed of her disease.

The constant flow of blood caused this woman to always feel weak. It was no wonder that she felt weak, since her blood was constantly carrying nutrients out of her body. The woman's illness caused her frustration; she had used all of her resources on doctor after doctor and on treatment after treatment—only to wake up day after day with the same challenge.

Because of her flow of blood, society viewed this woman as "unclean." She was therefore treated as an outcast. There were specific ritualistic rules related to her condition. Anything she touched was considered unclean; anyone who touched her or her possessions was considered unclean. People of both sexes viewed her as a *social* outcast as well; she was always alone, always struggling, always in a weak state. This disparaging treatment increased the woman's frustration and depression. Her illness took both a physical and an emotional toll on her. Twelve years can seem like a lifetime.

Putting Faith in Jesus

Then the woman heard about Jesus and the healing He was doing. She heard and she *believed*. Her hearing and believing caused her to act. In spite of her affliction—and *because* of her affliction—she resolved to get to Jesus. She thought that if she could just get to Him, she would be well.

But the obstacles were many. It would not be easy to get to Jesus in her weakened state. She'd need to push through the crowd as an outcast, breaking all social rules in one last hope for healing. And so she *did* make her way to Jesus—despite her weakened state, despite the crowd, and despite her social stigma.

The woman experienced a personal encounter with Jesus. Her objective had been to reach Jesus, and that she did! And that meeting with Jesus led to a miracle in her life: healing of an issue of blood that had plagued her life for twelve long years. The woman's struggle had led her to an action of desperate faith. Struggle can and should cause us to learn perseverance, should cause us to act on our faith and seek the Lord with a spirit of desperation.

In Psalm 63:1 David wrote the following:

O God, you are my God; earnestly I seek you;

my soul thirsts for you; my flesh faints for you, as in a dry

and weary land where there is no water.

It is that level of desperation and clarity of need that led this woman to seek out Jesus. And it is that level of desperation and clarity of need that can cause us to push through obstacles. Indeed, the woman let go of pride, and ignored social mores and physical obstacles to make contact with the Messiah.

Lessons Learned from Struggle

As a result of her struggle, the woman learned a number of vital lessons. Even before she met Jesus, she learned to focus during her struggle, to fix her face on the object of her faith and to push through. She learned to *act* on her faith; to move beyond mere *belief*, and to grasp her faith as reality.

From her short encounter with Jesus, the woman gained more than healing. She learned reverence. She believed that Jesus had the power to heal—that just touching Him would heal her. She came to see Jesus as the source of healing.

The woman learned that God is accessible if we approach Him with belief. She learned that faith can cause us to stretch, to push through, to assert a will to know God. She learned that people can touch an almighty God and that He does indeed know us. She learned that God has the power to heal, and that His healing is complete. She learned that God honors faithfulness.

What a climax to a twelve-year struggle! And what a testimony to all who had known her during her illness! I can imagine the marvel and the hope in the eyes of those who knew her. I can imagine the dialogue that took place and the joy of those who cared for her. But most of all, I can imagine the joy the woman must have felt. What had felt like a life (or death) sentence had been rescinded. And God had done it!

Even when a struggle seems endless, there is deliverance in Jesus!

Reflection to Strengthen You for Your Struggle
What was the woman's struggle?
What did the woman's struggle teach her about the nature of God?
What was the impact of woman's struggle on her?
What was the impact of the woman's struggle on others?
How does the woman's experience with God in her struggle
relate to your life?

Paul: Thorns and Imprisonment

Philippians 1

The Apostle Paul describes two simultaneous experiences with struggle: an external battle and an internal battle. Paul wrote his letter to the Philippians, as well as his other prison epistles, during his first imprisonment in Rome. Although he was guarded by soldiers, he was permitted to have many visitors and was given the opportunity to teach and preach to all who came to see him. During his time as a missionary, Paul had long desired to go to Rome, but his method of finally getting there illustrates yet another aspect of our struggles in life: Our struggles can provide opportunities for us to reach our long-sought goals. Our struggles can move us toward our destinies.

The Opportunity of Imprisonment

After being charged with blasphemy by Jewish officials, Paul defended himself by declaring his Roman citizenship and demanding to have his case heard by Caesar. As a citizen, he had that right. However, rather than arriving as a free missionary, able to move about the city freely, Paul arrived as a prisoner, surrounded by guards and restricted in movement. His future was uncertain; even the length of his prison sentence was indefinite. While he was imprisoned, however, Paul penned what would eventually become a significant portion of the New Testament.

In Philippians 1:12–20, Paul presents an intriguing perspective on his imprisonment.

[12] I want you to know, brothers, that what has happened to me has really served to advance the gospel, [13] so that it has become known throughout the whole imperial guard and to all the rest that my imprisonment is for Christ. [14] And most of the brothers, having become confident in the Lord by my imprisonment, are much more bold to speak the word without fear. [15] Some indeed preach Christ from envy and rivalry, but others from good will. [16] The latter do it out of love, knowing that I am put here for the defense of the gospel. [17] The former proclaim Christ out of selfish ambition, not sincerely but thinking to afflict me in my imprisonment. [18] What then? Only that in every way, whether in pretense or in truth, Christ is proclaimed, and in that I rejoice. Yes, and I will rejoice, [19] for I know that through your prayers and the help of the Spirit of Jesus Christ this will turn out for my deliverance, [20] as it is my eager expectation and hope that I will not be at all ashamed, but that with full courage now as always Christ will be honored in my body, whether by life or by death.

Paul's letter to his followers reveals the depths of his understanding of the impact of his struggle on others. It's as if he argues, "This is looking from a godly perspective: My visible struggle and my response to my challenge have led to nonbelievers seeing my firm witness, which glorifies God; and my struggle and response have led to believers like me being encouraged. My enemy has seen my faith and my conviction, which must be clear to onlookers. Believers who have seen me stand have become more confident in their own stand. People will respond to me in different ways, but that is not my concern. That is God's concern, and He will handle that."

This gets really personal for me as a believer. If God gets glory from my struggle, I should *rejoice*, but I know that rejoicing in struggle is impossible without the power of the Holy Spirit. Paul wanted God glorified in him—whether he lived or died. What an incredibly high standard for a person to live by—a standard that is impossible to achieve if one is not fully committed to "Christ and the faith," and impossible to achieve if one is not also empowered by the Holy Spirit. Who can say that being imprisoned would not be a struggle? Who can say that being lied to by those who profess to believe what you believe is not a struggle? Paul recognized the significance of the moment and his own human tendencies to begin to think more of himself than he should—to see himself as greater than others, perhaps more favored than others. Paul understood human nature, and he understood himself.

The Internal Struggle of Affliction

With the blessing of Paul's revelations from Jesus, came a personal affliction. Scholars have argued for years about the nature of Paul's affliction. Was it a physical deformity? Was it a psychological issue? Was it epilepsy? Was it the continuous torment of enemies? Rather than trying to determine the nature of Paul's challenge, I want to look at the challenge's impact on Paul, and at the purpose Paul saw in this affliction. Paul's words in 2 Corinthians 12: 7–10 describe his response best:

> 7 So to keep me from becoming conceited because of
> the surpassing greatness of the revelations, a thorn was
> given me in the flesh, a messenger of Satan to harass me,
> to keep me from becoming conceited. 8 Three times I
> pleaded with the Lord about this, that it should leave
> me. 9 But He said to me, "My grace is sufficient for you,
> for my power is made perfect in weakness." Therefore I
> will boast all the more gladly of my weaknesses, so that the
> power of Christ may rest upon me. 10 For the sake of

Christ, then, I am content with weaknesses, insults, hardships, persecutions, and calamities. For when I am weak, then I am strong.

Paul perceived that the glories he had experienced were beyond the experiences of others, and he boasted about them. Yet Paul also understood that God had to do something to him to keep him focused on the main thing—God—and not himself. God gave Paul a torment, something to buffet him in life, to keep him struggling, to keep him praying. Three times Paul appealed to God for the thorn to be removed—but God said no.

God Himself clarified the reason: Paul had to come to understand that the grace of God was sufficient to protect him, even with an ongoing struggle. Paul learned the meaning of sufficient grace, of ever-available grace that would allow him to persevere through opposition. In Philippians 4:11 Paul states, "I have learned in whatever situation I am to be content." I have no doubt that Paul was referring here to the process of continuing to fight through his struggle, even celebrating the struggle because it revealed more of God's nature and power to him.

God's Prerogative — and Our Response

God doesn't always deliver us from our issues. Sometimes He uses an issue to teach us what we need to know, to prepare us for what is ahead of us in life. Our struggle may be internal or external. The struggle may last for a season as Paul's imprisonment did, or it may be with us for a lifetime, as his affliction was.

We may pray and pray for relief, and God may be silent or may give us a distinct "No!" God's "No" becomes a roadmap to our experiencing greater depths of His love and grace. In the end, what God always desires of us is that we spend more time in relationship with Him. When we are eagerly awaiting the Lord's response, we tend to be in an active listening mode, and that time becomes a season of meditation and consecration.

In both his imprisonment and his struggle with the thorn, Paul clearly models for us the mindset of rejoicing in the midst of our challenge or restrictions. Only the Spirit of God can empower us to do that.

Reflection to Strengthen You for Your Struggle
What were Paul's struggles?
What did Paul's struggles teach him about the nature of God?
What was the impact of Paul's struggles on him?
What was the impact of Paul's struggle on others?
How does Paul's experience with God in his struggles relate to your life?

The Struggling Church

Acts 4 and 8

The book of Acts offers many narratives about the struggles to begin a new faith, a new Church. The Apostles regularly got into conflict with religious leaders. There were two basic sources of this conflict: who the Apostles were, and what they preached. Religious leaders looked down on the Apostles, who lacked the formal religious training to which synagogue leaders and local scholars were accustomed. In addition, religious leaders found the Apostles' message—of Jesus' resurrection—intolerable. Ultimately this conflict led to the arrest and detention of Peter and John in Jerusalem.

Despite frequent conflict, the Apostles' impact on the masses was undeniable. Follow this narrative from Acts 4:1–28 as it unfolds:

> [1]And as they were speaking to the people, the priests and the captain of the temple and the Sadducees came upon them, [2] greatly annoyed because they were teaching the people and proclaiming in Jesus the resurrection from the dead. [3] And they arrested them and put them in custody until the next day, for it was already evening. [4] But many of those who had heard the word believed, and the number of the men came to about five thousand.
>
> [5] On the next day their rulers and elders and scribes gathered together in Jerusalem, [6] with Annas the high priest and Caiaphas and John and Alexander, and all who were of the high-priestly family. [7] And when they had set

them in the midst, they inquired, "By what power or by what name did you do this?"

8 Then Peter, filled with the Holy Spirit, said to them, "Rulers of the people and elders, 9 if we are being examined today concerning a good deed done to a crippled man, by what means this man has been healed, 10 let it be known to all of you and to all the people of Israel that by the name of Jesus Christ of Nazareth, whom you crucified, whom God raised from the dead—by Him this man is standing before you well. 11 This Jesus is the stone that was rejected by you, the builders, which has become the cornerstone. 12 And there is salvation in no one else, for there is no other name under heaven given among men by which we must be saved."

13 Now when they saw the boldness of Peter and John, and perceived that they were uneducated, common men, they were astonished. And they recognized that they had been with Jesus. 14 But seeing the man who was healed standing beside them, they had nothing to say in opposition. 15 But when they had commanded them to leave the council, they conferred with one another, 16 saying, "What shall we do with these men? For that a notable sign has been performed through them is evident to all the inhabitants of Jerusalem, and we cannot deny it. 17 But in order that it may spread no further among the people, let us warn them to speak no more to anyone in this name."

18 So they called them and charged them not to speak or teach at all in the name of Jesus. 19 But Peter and John answered them, "Whether it is right in the sight of God to listen to you rather than to God, you must judge, 20 for we cannot but speak of what we have seen and heard." 21 And when they had further threatened them, they let them go,

finding no way to punish them, because of the people, for all were praising God for what had happened. 22 For the man on whom this sign of healing was performed was more than forty years old.

23 When they were released, they went to their friends and reported what the chief priests and the elders had said to them. 24 And when they heard it, they lifted their voices together to God and said, "Sovereign Lord, who made the heaven and the earth and the sea and everything in them, 25 who through the mouth of our father David, your servant, said by the Holy Spirit,

"'Why did the Gentiles rage, and the peoples plot in vain? 26 The kings of the earth set themselves, and the rulers were gathered together, against the Lord and against His Anointed'— 27 for truly in this city there were gathered together against your holy servant Jesus, whom you anointed, both Herod and Pontius Pilate, along with the Gentiles and the peoples of Israel, 28 to do whatever your hand and your plan had predestined to take place.

God's Hand in the Struggle

The previous passage concludes with a powerful biblical principle that serves to inform us and equip us to face whatever struggle or storm is before us. Verse 28 says that the actions taken by the enemy, first against Jesus and later against the Apostles, were taken because of God's hand (His power) and God's purpose (His plan). *Our struggles occur within the power and purpose of God.*

And yet we can still pray during the struggle. Acts 4:29–31 helps us know what to pray for:

29 And now, Lord, look upon their threats and grant to your servants to continue to speak your word with all boldness, 30 while you stretch out your hand to heal, and signs and wonders are performed through the name of

your holy servant Jesus." [31] And when they had prayed, the
place in which they were gathered together was shaken,
and they were all filled with the Holy Spirit and continued
to speak the word of God with boldness.

These disciples did not ask for deliverance, for mercy, for peace.
Instead they asked for more power from God to heal and to do
signs and wonders that would point the people to God! They still
saw the power source being Jesus Christ. And what was the result of
this unselfish prayer? Boldness in the preaching of the gospel.

The Opportunity in Persecution

The early church grew in an environment of struggle and adversity.
It is much like what is going on in the twenty-first century. The
church is thriving in places where persecution is intense. Why is
that? What is the value of the struggle of these believers? From the
history of the New Testament, it seems that struggle fuels
conviction for the believer. It inspires obedience in the face of
challenge. It keeps people engaged with God through prayer.

In such cases, the actual struggle, the actual persecution, pushes
believers out of their comfort zone and into places where they'll
have opportunities to share the gospel. A look at Acts 8:1–4 makes
this abundantly clear:

[1]And Saul approved of his execution. And there arose
on that day a great persecution against the church in
Jerusalem, and they were all scattered throughout the
regions of Judea and Samaria, except the apostles.
[2] Devout men buried Stephen and made great lamentation
over him. [3] But Saul was ravaging the church, and entering
house after house, he dragged off men and women and
committed them to prison.
[4] Now those who were scattered went about
preaching the word.

As a result of the struggle, the church was pushed out of Jerusalem, literally. But look at the Apostles' response. Yes, they left! Yes, they became refugees! Yes, they were dispersed—but everywhere they went, they preached Jesus! The Great Commission, recorded in Matthew 8:19–20, was now being carried out by the masses:

> [19] "Go therefore and make disciples of all nations, baptizing them in the name of the Father and of the Son and of the Holy Spirit, [20] teaching them to observe all that I have commanded you. And behold, I am with you always, to the end of the age."

The Apostles' natural response to the struggle of their circumstances was to flee—and that very action led directly to their obedience to the Great Commission. The inherent power of struggle, adversity, and storms in our lives is that those difficulties cause us to leave our comfort zones, as if pushed from a nest. Struggles cause us to clarify our Bible-based beliefs—and act on them! Struggles cause us to face impossible odds with a mind to be obedient to God. They reveal the power of God, the heart of God, the purposes of God, and the sovereignty of God in our lives. If we would truly embrace the struggle as the Apostles did following Peter's and John's release, the power of God could be manifested in ways we cannot currently imagine.

If our struggles are designed and controlled by God for our development, then it makes sense that we should learn to embrace them, learn from them, and grow so that we will be more effective disciples of Christ.

I won't claim that any of this is easy. That would be insulting to any reader. This study is about the clarity and power that are inherent in our experiences with our struggles. It's about coming to know, through our struggles, the God who created us. It's about growing and developing, and daily being shaped into the image and likeness of Christ.

Peter's and John's stand in their struggle with the Sanhedrin caused the Apostles to continue to praise God and to become bolder in their own stand. The foundation of the Church as a community of believers took form out of their stand of faith. Their courage and commitment challenged others to do the same, and the Church continued its growth. Similarly, the stand we take in our own struggles serves to embolden us and to encourage others in the faith. Our struggles are seldom about us alone. We must be prepared to struggle alone and with others, and—for the sake of all—to persist in our struggle as long as there is need.

Reflection to Strengthen You for Your Struggle
What was the Church's struggle?
What did the Church learn in this struggle about the nature of God?
How did the struggle of the early Church impact the Church itself?
What was the impact of the early Church's struggle on others?
How does the Church's experience with God in his struggle relate to your life?

Embracing the Struggle

Matthew 26:36–44

For someone to embrace a struggle—to willingly move toward something that is difficult, to grab hold of something that will hurt—requires a supernatural drive. It isn't a natural response for any of us to run toward something that may be painful, and that may ultimately be personally destructive.

Jesus in the Garden of Gethsemane

The time immediately preceding Jesus' arrest, recorded in Matthew 26:36–44, perfectly illustrates the concept of "embracing the struggle."

> 36 Then Jesus went with them to a place called Gethsemane, and He said to His disciples, "Sit here, while I go over there and pray." 37 And taking with Him Peter and the two sons of Zebedee, He began to be sorrowful and troubled. 38 Then He said to them, "My soul is very sorrowful, even to death; remain here, and watch with me." 39 And going a little farther He fell on His face and prayed, saying, "My Father, if it be possible, let this cup pass from me; nevertheless, not as I will, but as you will."
>
> 40 And He came to the disciples and found them sleeping. And He said to Peter, "So, could you not watch with me one hour? 41 Watch and pray that you may not enter into temptation. The spirit indeed is willing, but the flesh is weak." 42 Again, for the second time, He went

away and prayed, "My Father, if this cannot pass unless I drink it, your will be done." [43] And again He came and found them sleeping, for their eyes were heavy. [44] So, leaving them again, He went away and prayed for the third time, saying the same words again.

Jesus stood alone in the garden, staring down at the sleeping men who had accompanied Him on the ultimate journey of faith. They were totally exhausted, physically drained, and emotionally weak. They were His Apostles, His inner circle. These were men who had seen the miracles, heard the teaching, and experienced the full range of drama that came with following the Messiah.

Twice Jesus came to them, imploring them to be vigilant as He prayed, as He prepared for the event that would represent the fulfillment of His earthly mission. His was an all-night vigil, praying to His Father in Heaven about the turmoil and torture of the next day, praying until sweat like drops of blood flowed from His face and dropped to the ground. Jesus knew what was about to occur. He knew exactly what His future held. And the man in the God-Man was wrestling with the idea that He must endure that agony.

As Jesus knelt, He cried out to the Father. A paraphrase of His prayer might sound something like this: "If it be your will, remove this cup of suffering from my future! Change my destiny! Give me another direction to travel! I know what this path will hold for me—supreme suffering! Not just the pain and agony of nails in my hands, a spear in my side, lashes on my back amid a horrible beating. No, even more painful than all of that will be the moment on the cross when I take on the sins of this world and pay the highest possible price for that sin—losing fellowship with you!"

Jesus as Our Model

Despite Jesus' initial reluctance to embrace His mission, eventually He models for us the very nature we must emulate if we are to be effective as believers. As a teacher, I can attest to the power of modeling as the most effective strategy for teaching. When a teacher demonstrates how a task is to be done—fully pouring himself into the lesson—students get to experience the full scope of the act: the mental discipline, the physical action, the evident consuming passion about the significance of the act, the satisfaction of the final product.

Jesus, as the quintessential teacher, shows each of us what it means to embrace the struggle. As we see in Matthew 16:24, He had already taught His Apostles, "If anyone would come after me, let him deny himself and take up his cross and follow me." As He now presents Himself as a living sacrifice, what does His modeling of sacrifice imply for us?

God's call on our life is large. God's calling on our life is larger than *we* ourselves can envision, and it often causes us to struggle. Although we have the gifts to be effective, that doesn't mean that what we have to face will naturally appeal to us. Although our calling is worthy and righteous, that doesn't mean that we'll escape struggle or sacrifice.

We'll often have to stand alone. When we're faced with an extremely difficult struggle, there may be people around us who ought to be able to stand with us, but they are just not able to do so. It isn't a condition of their heart that causes them to let us down; rather they may just be exhausted, they may have nothing left to give at that moment. The experiences of life itself may have impacted them in such a way that they are just not able to be present for us. In such a moment, each of us will need to stand alone.

Persistent prayer is required. When we finally realize that we must go through a struggle alone, we must do what Jesus did: persistently pray to God. We must ask God to make His will our will. We must say what we feel in our heart; then we must stay in prayer until we feel our will submit to the will of God. We must be persistent. This is not a polite prayer, a public liturgy, or a ritualistic exercise; this is the height of supplication—asking God to do something specific for us, pleading with God to meet a felt need, to empower us to complete what He has laid on our heart to do.

We must embrace the will of God. In Luke 22:42 we again see Jesus asking God to make His upcoming suffering unnecessary: "Father, if you are willing, remove this cup from me. Nevertheless, not my will, but yours, be done." Persistent prayer and faith in God will take believers to the point where we can finally say to God, "I am yours. Do with me as you desire. Just give me the strength to stand— and to remain standing when this struggle is over."

By the time Judas and the squadron of soldiers arrived to take Jesus prisoner, the man in the God-Man was embracing the culmination of this phase of His ministry. His demeanor indicated His assertive acceptance of the situation and of the challenge that lay ahead of Him. He awakened His Apostles, simply saying, "The hour is at hand, and the Son of Man is betrayed into the hands of sinners" (Matthew 26:45b).

Embracing God's will in our struggles not only equips us; it empowers us to face whatever the ensuing struggle holds.

Our Benefits from Jesus' Mission

As we have done with all of the other people whose lives we've examined in this study, we must explore the benefits of what Jesus did in completing His divine mission. Because of what He did, we are now declared righteous before God. Our salvation is sure. Our faith is unshaken. We have power to live our lives victoriously. Because of what Jesus did in the garden and on the cross, we have hope. Because of what He did, the Apostles could boldly go and lay down their lives for the cause of the cross, the faith, and the Church. Jesus' actions empowered them with courage for their ministries.

Because of what Jesus did in embracing the struggle that night in the garden, we can access the same power that He had. As Jesus said, recorded in John 14:12, "Truly, truly, I say to you, whoever believes in me will also do the works that I do; and greater works than these will he do, because I am going to the Father."

Reflection to Strengthen You for Your Struggle
What was Jesus' struggle?
What was the impact of Jesus' struggle on Him?
What was the impact of Jesus' struggle on others?
How does Jesus' experience with God in His struggle relate to your life?

Struggling to See God in Chaos: An Application

People around the world faced unimagined challenges in 2020. The United States of America, accustomed to resourcefully meeting any adversity that presented itself, was suddenly floundering on multiple fronts, including an uncontrollable pandemic and simultaneously escalating racial strife. These issues plagued individual citizens and the country as a whole.

Crippled by a Pandemic

In November 2020 the world was gripped in the throes of a pandemic. Millions of people were infected. Hundreds of thousands of people in the United States had died. What appeared to be "common sense" precautions had been politicized to the point that something as simple as wearing a mask to cover one's mouth and nose became recognized as a litmus test of patriotism, loyalty to the sitting president of the United States, value of individual liberties, and/or faith in God. Millions of people rejected the ideas of mask-wearing, social distancing, and avoiding high-risk gatherings. The number of cases of COVID-19 continued to climb with the onset of winter. Because new details about the virus were continuously emerging, because the flu season was rapidly approaching, and because a new surge of the virus was under way (not to mention the fact that millions of people had lost their jobs and didn't have enough money to buy food for their families), a sense of chaos and disorder pervaded the country.

By January 2021, the death toll in the United States from COVID-19 had risen to 433,000. Approximately 3,000 people in the country were dying each day, and 25.8 million people had been infected. Around the world new strains of the virus developed. There was a constant ebb and flow of the illness, depending upon geographic location and upon holidays or other events that caused people to gather in large groups. Vaccines, which became available in December offered a glimmer of hope, even as the winter season promised more suffering.

Distribution of the vaccine proved to be more challenging than anticipated. Often states didn't know how much vaccine they'd get or when they'd receive it. Hence, scheduling appointments and ensuring that doses of vaccine could be administered before their expiration date became difficult.

Wrestling with Racial Injustice and Conflict

On May 25, 2020, the cry "Black Lives Matter!" took on an escalated level of urgency when the world, in shock, watched a video of a policeman kneeling on the neck of an African American man in custody on a city street. The policeman kept kneeling on his neck even though the man said he couldn't breathe and onlookers helplessly pleaded for his life. The policeman knelt on the man's neck until the struggle ceased, until the man's pulse ceased.

The death of George Floyd, presented in real time for the world to witness and experience over and over again, provoked a worldwide response. The video galvanized sentiment across racial, socioeconomic, educational, ethnic, and nationalistic lines. It laid bare to many what the African American community had for generations been experiencing and feeling about its relationship with law enforcement. Multiethnic groups around the globe took to the streets in peaceful demonstrations. Calls for police reform and cries of "Defund the police!" echoed. The cry for racial justice and an end to brutality rooted in the racialized history of America, the Thirteenth Amendment, segregation, and white supremacy all boiled up at once.

Almost immediately after the chants of "Black Lives Matter!" filled the air, other voices began to counter that message with "Blue Lives Matter!"—the lives of policemen mattered. Several individuals sought vengeance on individual policemen through targeted shootings. Civilian and police videos and reports of incidents continued to spotlight the stark disparity between the treatment of African Americans in custody and the treatment of whites in custody.

Ninety-four percent of Black Lives Matter protests were peaceful, but there was violence from an active minority who chose not to follow a nonviolent approach. That minority, and the violence they caused, contributed to misinformation about both the protests and the protestors. In addition, other groups who advocated anarchy and "racial war" joined the Black Lives Matter protests, dangerously fueling the controversy.

Where Is God in All of This?
A pandemic that has killed hundreds of thousands of people in the United States. The agonizing public death of an unarmed man at the knee of a law enforcement officer.

Where is God in all of this? How can a person see the hand of God in such events? How can an individual believer, molded by his or her own life experiences and conditioned by his or her own racial experience, see God's hand and apply the teachings of Christ to his perceptions of others?

These events crystallized a reality for me as I participated in a Bible study with believers from several local churches. Responses to each of the circumstances discussed in this chapter were as divergent among believers as they were among nonbelievers. How can that be when we all declare a love of the Word of God and an allegiance to the teachings of Christ? How can two groups of believers view the same event—and one group recognizes injustice in the event and the other does not? Or how can one group of believers see injustice but not understand the pain of a brother or sister? What do we need to understand to truly experience God in each of these collective struggles? What do we need to be learning?

To discover this answer, I began to reflect upon each of these challenges—the pandemic, and the racial confrontation. While these challenges were occurring simultaneously, it helped me to first consider them individually.

What Can We Learn About God in a Crippling Pandemic?

The pandemic crossed all manmade barriers—race, class, socioeconomics, nationalistic allegiances, religion, gender, and age. It impacted developed as well as developing countries. In doing this, the pandemic highlighted the huge gap between the haves and the have-nots. Poorer communities initially suffered greater loss of life in the pandemic because of poorer health among the community members and fewer available healthcare options. As schools shifted to virtual platforms, the disparity of resources between affluent and poorer districts—urban, suburban, and rural—became more evident.

Many leaders on multiple levels began to use the COVID precautions advocated by experts to create a litmus test for both patriotism and faith. The result had individuals fighting each other over the best way to protect themselves, or arguing as to whether any protection was even needed. Others staunchly denied the very existence of the pandemic, even as death tolls climbed.

The faith community was divided as well. Many church leaders, believing that the Word of God called the people of God to physically assemble no matter what, continued to meet face to face. As local governing bodies began to implement stringent policies about social gatherings, several churches openly defied those policies, viewing them as a direct assault on their civil liberties. Some prominent church leaders actually took cases to court. For many of the church congregations who continued to meet in person without strict adherence to precautions, the number of people infected increased, sometimes resulting in the loss of many lives. People suffered emotionally and psychologically from separation when churches did close their physical doors.

Yet many churches used this struggle as an opportunity to pivot. They began to hold virtual services. They developed strategies using technology in ways that suddenly enabled them to make the gospel available to audiences even larger than those they'd had before the pandemic. The number of online worship services and Bible studies increased. People who had mastered skill in using these platforms in their day-to-day work began to use their skill to spread the gospel in a new way. Both new technology and simple conference calls that allowed people to come together in prayer made many people realize that God-given tools can provide man with the ability to create more effective ways to minister.

Believers began to act on a new reality: They began to recognize the "Church" as the body of believers, not the church building. With this recognition came the realization that even though they could not assemble in a traditional manner—they could still assemble virtually, call the elderly, shop for those who may be quarantined. They learned that the Great Commission could be carried out using contemporary tools. It taught them that they needed to actually demonstrate love for communities that had a much smaller supply of resources than they themselves had.

What did we believers learn about God and the Church? God reminded us that He is sovereign. He orchestrates. He heals. He challenges us to know Him more deeply through adversity. We learned that the Body of Christ can overcome obstacles in order to still engage in fellowship. It was as if God used the struggle of COVID-19 to prune us of some non-essentials—buildings, huge gatherings, long ornate ceremonies—and to lead us back to viewing the home as a place of intimate worship. It was if God was saying,

"You have become too distracted. I need your full attention. When I have your full attention, your full trust, then I will show my power."

What did we learn about ourselves as individuals? We learned that spending more time in the Word of God and in prayer is critical to our peace of mind. We learned that God is with us when we suffer from the illness and are healed, *and* when we have lost a loved one. God's Spirit is always there to comfort us. We learned that God is still in charge of timing as the vaccine was rolled out expeditiously—and we reminded ourselves of God's sovereignty when distribution of the vaccine proved to be more challenging than was expected. We learned that we still have to take action based upon faith as we decide whether or not to get the vaccine. We learned amid a pandemic that God will keep us in perfect peace if we keep our minds focused on Him.

What Can We Learn About God Amid Racial Unrest?

The idea of race is so deeply embedded in the fiber of the United States—historic slavery, enslaved Africans being declared in the Constitution to be three-fifths of a human, emancipation, Reconstruction, Jim Crow, segregation, desegregation, integration, Civil Rights, voting rights, resegregation rooted in economic disparity—the struggle and counter-struggle seem never-ending. Given such a background, how do we see God in the midst of our struggles over racial injustice, even racial conflict? How do believers from different cultural, ethnic, and racial backgrounds reconcile experiencing different interpretations and different feelings sparked by the same event?

I contend that the fact that so many people—across all kinds of cultural lines—were equally horrified by the death of George Floyd was God at work. Many people in society had considered "racial injustice" only as an abstract idea. With the killing of George Floyd, that concept immediately became concrete. God touched hearts to be more compassionate, and He challenged closed minds to actually

117

consider the idea of empathy. Whites who frequently doubted the veracity of black voices warning of a double standard in the justice system began to find truth in what they were hearing.

God confronted the intellectual arguments often posed when an African American dies in custody—the person of color "did something wrong," which caused him or her to be killed by law enforcement. The killing of George Floyd caused many church congregations to become more acutely aware of how they treat people who are considered the "others." In many ways the churches reflected the culture around them.

Revelation 7:9 became a focal point for many congregations.

> After this I looked, and behold, a great multitude that
> no one could number, from every nation, from all tribes
> and peoples and languages, standing before the throne and
> before the Lamb, clothed in white robes, with palm
> branches in their hands.

God describes His Church as a great multitude of people who are socially, ethnically, racially, and culturally distinct individuals, yet share a common focus on God and His truth. He permitted chaos, personal tragedy, and social unrest to challenge believers to see each other the way He sees us. He used the events of multiple deaths, and the brutal conversations about racial healing that followed, to provoke change in hearts and minds.

When it comes to addressing the concept of race, the great challenge of the Church is to love as Christ loved: To love through difference; to value differences as the handiwork of God; and to value distinction in the same manner that God the Creator values distinction.

Experiencing God in Chaos

How do we experience God in chaos?

- We seek God's presence with the intent of discerning His hand at work in all events.

- We intentionally take action that aspires to align with the revealed principles of God's Word, and we help others to do the same.
- We consider decisions that we're making, and use God's Word as a template by which to judge the value and purpose of what we say and do.
- We look at the actions of others in light of the character that God calls believers to exhibit.
- We grasp the challenge of loving an enemy—one who has practiced deceit, has deliberately spread lies, has overtly threatened physical harm to us and to others, has expressed racial hatred, or has used a position of power to do evil.
- We pray for the power to love those who hate, to protect those we love, to declare truth to those who are lost.
- We feed ourselves with the Word of God, choosing not to live on a diet of reports of chaos and carnage.
- We examine our own heart so that we do not fall into our own cycle of hate and despair.
- We remind ourselves of God's promises, including the one He gives us in Romans 8:28—"And we know that for those who love God all things work together for good, for those who are called according to His purpose."

We look for the good, the productive, the lessons God is teaching us in the pandemic, the racial conflicts, and the political discord and unrest. We look for guidance in what the Word of God says about justice, and about loving our brothers and sisters *and* our enemies. We understand that God calls us to act because of who we are. We understand that in all things—even in chaos—God still has plans for our lives.

Reflection to Strengthen You for Your Struggle

This chapter has focused upon two events that people in the United States concurrently experienced. Reflect on the following questions in relation to each event.

What was the Church's struggle in each of these events?

What was the nation's struggle in each of the events?

What is revealed about the nature of God in each of the struggles?

What did you learn about yourself during these struggles?

Helping Nonbelievers in Their Struggle

2 Chronicles 7:14

How can imperfect believers, with their own struggles and their own prejudices, actually impact the world? God provides insight to this in 2 Chronicles 7:14.

> If my people who are called by my name humble themselves, and pray and seek my face and turn from their wicked ways, then I will hear from heaven and will forgive their sin and heal their land.

This analysis is straightforward:

We must first recognize that we are God's people, called by Him, named by Him, and claimed by Him. Our relationship with Him is personal. Our relationship is with a God who revealed Himself as a man in the incarnation of Jesus the Christ. Jesus then revealed God's ultimate relationship with us by dying on a cross for the sins of all people who recognize Him as their Lord and Savior.

As God's people, we must develop a sense of humility. We are the created, not the creator. In God, we live, move, and have our being.

We must pray. Prayer is a dialogue with God. We can boldly approach God with our heartfelt praise, worship, and specific petitions. But after we say our prayers, we must stay at the altar and listen to God's response. If His response is to wait, then we are to wait faithfully, working in place until more direction is offered.

We must actively pursue a relationship with God through study and meditation. This means spending time before the face of God as openly and honestly as we can.

We must repent of our sins. We must honestly acknowledge where we have fallen short, commit to changing, and ask God for the strength to change. In this same vein, we must thank God for the grace and mercy that He daily provides to us.

These steps are a prerequisite that the body of believers must meet before the fallen world can be expected to experience any healing. The steps will compel us to see God in whatever struggles we face. His Word lays out the order of the steps and tells us the outcome of taking these steps. The outcome is forgiven sins, and the healing and restoration of the people and the conditions of the land.

Conclusion

As you read this book, did you identify with some people and their struggles more than with others? Reflecting on struggles that are most similar to your own may help you develop some strategies that will enable you to engage, even *embrace*, your struggles more effectively.

Consider the Nature of Your Own Struggles

You might begin by considering the following questions:

- Is your struggle a "David" situation, where you're facing a giant in life? If so, remember the other giants you've faced and what you've learned from those encounters.

- Is your struggle a "Jonah" situation, where you're wrapped up in the consequences of your own poor decision-making? If so, remember that this is a time for you to reconnect to the core principles that have sustained you, to reconnect to the God who made you.

- Is your struggle an "Esther" situation, where you have to step outside yourself in order to take a principled stand for others? If so, remember that your stand matters to the lives of others, and that one of God's important purposes for your life might involve taking a decisive stand in one moment!

- Is your struggle a "Daniel" situation, in which case you must know that your struggle is going to affect the lives of others and renew your own commitment as you go to higher levels in your relationship with God?

124

Perhaps there were other people written about in this book whose struggles seemed to more closely resemble yours. Review those chapters, thinking more about those struggles and what you might learn from them.

Press On with Your Own Struggles

We should respond to our struggles as Paul describes in Philippians 3:13b–14: "Forgetting what lies behind and straining forward to what lies ahead, I press on toward the goal for the prize of the upward call of God in Christ Jesus." We press on because there is purpose in our struggles. We move forward because God uses our struggles to mold us and shape us. We remain diligent because God has promised that He will never leave us or forsake us. We press on because God has promised that He has begun a good work in us and that He will complete it! We press on because we are made in the image and likeness of our creator, and He took the form of man, came to this world, and struggled on our behalf—so that we might know that He knows our struggles and intimately knows us.

Here are some references if you'd like to read more about the concepts mentioned in the previous paragraph:

- Purpose in our struggles: 2 Corinthians 1:8–11; 2 Corinthians 12: 7–10; Philippians 1:12–14; Philippians 2:13
- God using our struggles to mold and shape us: Jonah 2:1–10; Romans 3–5; 2 Corinthians 12:7–10; Philippians 2:13; James 1:2–4
- God's promise to be with us always: Deuteronomy 31:8; Psalm 34:4; Psalm 55:22; Psalm 139:7–13; Isaiah 41:10; Isaiah 43:1–4; John 14:19; Romans 8:38–39; Hebrews 13:5; 1 Peter 5:6–10
- God's promise that He will complete a good work in us: Jeremiah 29:11–13; Ephesians 2:10; Philippians 1:6; 1 Peter 5:10

- Our being made in the image and likeness of God: Genesis 1:26–27; Genesis 2:7; Genesis 2:21–22; 1 Corinthians 3:16–18
- Jesus' struggling on our behalf: Matthew 26:38–44; Matthew 26:67–68; Matthew 27:28–50; 2 Corinthians 5:21; Hebrews 2:9–10

Review and Apply What You've Learned

As you think about the principles presented in this book, answer the following questions as a means of reviewing what you've learned.

- What did each person learn about God?
- What was developed in the life of the believer during the struggle?
- What did others (nonbelievers) who witnessed the struggle learn about God?

Now consider how you might *apply* what you've learned. If you're currently involved in a struggle, reflect on the following questions:

- What is your attitude toward your struggle?
- What actions, if any, are you taking as you deal with your struggle?
- Do you see your struggle as part of your growth process, or do you see it as some evil thing that Satan has brought upon you?
- Are you engaged in learning as you struggle, or are you just waiting for the struggle to end and for the sunshine to return?

Cultivate Your Relationship with God

In addition to the reflective activities mentioned above, regularly spending time in activities that will enhance your spiritual growth will not only prepare you to meet future struggles, but will also help you to be victorious in them. Such activities are equivalent to the training and strengthening exercises that help an athlete develop and maintain a strong body. Consider committing to the following:

- Read the Word of God to remind yourself that struggle is not new.
- Read stories of God's interactions with people in Scripture. Determine if your situation is similar to theirs. Learn from the experience of others who have struggled.
- Remember that God is purposeful in all that He does.
- Look for God's presence during your challenge.
- Ask yourself, "What should I learn about God as I struggle?"
- Pray persistently to feel God's presence during your struggle. Sometimes we may not need to ask Him to end the struggle, but rather to protect us and to make us aware of His presence during the struggle.

After you've resolved a challenge, reflect on your experience so that you'll be more prepared for future challenges.

- Determine where the true struggle lies. Was it more of an external challenge or an internal challenge?
- Meditate on the experience you had during your struggle. Give yourself some time to think and pray. Journal if you can. Write down your ideas so that you can return to them from time to time with new revelations about your experience.
- Ask yourself, "What do I now know about God, that I didn't know before?"
- Ask yourself, "What did I learn about myself and my level of faith?"
- Now that you know what you know, what will you do differently in the future? How will this new awareness impact your life?

Then go out and live that life!

Charles J. Pearson

Acknowledgments

Completing this book has been a long, yet rewarding process. It required me to reflect about challenging experiences that I have had as an adult and what I learned from each of those experiences. The process required me to pull together the many Biblical lessons I have taught and connect those to my own life. The common element of my experiences, my teaching, and my reflection has been the love and presence of my amazing wife, Betty.

Betty listened to my ideas, brainstormed with me on the big themes, proofread the manuscript multiple times and provided me great feedback as a reader of the book. She simultaneously probed my thinking and provided help with the "wordsmithing." Her support was vital to my completing this dream.

Betty, thank you for being a phenomenal wife and best friend.

I also thank Bishop Michael Fulton Jones, Sr. for his unwavering friendship and encouragement as I completed this book. His enthusiasm compelled me to get this finished so I could share the thinking—my voice-- with a wider audience. Bishop, thank you for your enduring brotherhood.

About the Author

Charles Pearson is Executive Pastor at the Friendly Temple MB Church, a thriving urban ministry. He has been an avid teacher of Biblical principles and their applications in life for over 30 years. Through his teaching at Adult and Youth Bible Studies, Men's Conferences, and Church Leadership Conferences, he continues to equip people to live impactful lives.

In writing *God, I'm Struggling,* he presents Biblical principles to a wider audience, drawing upon both his professional experience as an educational leader and a teacher. Charles and his family live in St. Louis, Missouri. To connect with Charles, please visit www.impactfulliving.org.

Dear Reader,

Thank you for reading *God, I'm Struggling.* I hope that you found it both helpful and insightful as you face, and reflect, upon your own struggles in life. It's all about understanding the purpose of God in your challenges. Learning from your experiences strengthens you in life.

If you found this book helpful, please consider posting a review online or your favorite store site. Even a few sentences would be much appreciated.

I would love to hear your thoughts about what you have learned about God and yourself during crises. I believe that our shared stories can encourage others who are experiencing their own challenges. *By sharing, we create community.*

Please email me at impactfulliving5@gmail.com or visit my website www.impactfulliving.net

Gratefully Yours,
Charles J. Pearson

Made in the USA
Monee, IL
22 January 2022